LÍLIA MOMPLÉ w
Mozambique and d
She was Secretary (
Association from 1995 to 2001 and President from 1997 to
1999. She has also represented her country at a number of
international cultural assemblies, and has recently been
appointed to the UNESCO Executive Council. Her publications
include *No One Killed Suhura* (1988), *The Eyes of the Green
Cobra* (1997) and the script for the award-winning
Mozambican video drama *Muhupitit Alima* (1988).
Neighbours was first published, in Portuguese, in 1995. Lília
Momplé lives with her husband in Maputo, the capital of
Mozambique.

RICHARD BARTLETT is a journalist working in
Johannesburg, South Africa. He has been studying the literature
of Mozambique for the past decade. His translations of
Mozambican short stories have appeared in a number of
anthologies and he edited *Short Stories from Mozambique*
(Cosaw, 1995).

ISAURA DE OLIVEIRA is based in Lisbon. She teaches
Portuguese language and literature. She spent six years as the
first Portuguese lecturer of the Instituto Camões at
Witwatersrand University in South Africa.

LÍLIA MOMPLÉ

NEIGHBOURS
THE STORY OF A MURDER

Translated by Richard Bartlett and Isaura de Oliveira

Heinemann

Heinemann Educational Publishers
Halley Court, Jordan Hill, Oxford OX2 8EJ
A Division of Reed Educational & Professional Publishing Ltd

Heinemann: A Division of Reed Publishing (USA) Inc.
361 Hanover Street, Portsmouth, NH 03801–3912, USA

Heinemann Publishers (Pty) Limited
PO Box 781940, Sandton 2146, Johannesburgh, South Africa

OXFORD   MELBOURNE   AUCKLAND
JOHANNESBURG   BLANTYRE   GABORONE
IBADAN   PORTSMOUTH (NH) USA   CHICAGO

Available in Zimbabwe from Weaver Press

First published by Heinemann Educational Publishers in 2001

British Library Cataloguing in Publication Data
A catalogue record for this book is available from the British Library.

AFRICAN WRITERS SERIES and CARIBBEAN WRITERS SERIES and
their accompanying logos are trademarks in the United States of America
of Heinemann: A Division of Reed Publishing (USA) Inc.

Cover design by Amanda Carroll
Cover illustration by Malangatana

Phototypeset by SetSystems Ltd, Saffron Walden, Essex
Printed and bound in Great Britain by
Cox and Wyman Ltd, Reading, Berkshire

ISBN 0 435 91209 7

01 02 03 04 05 06 07 08 8 7 6 5 4 3 2 1

Preface

Oppression can take many forms. *Neighbours* was written out of my horror at the way countries can abuse each other's sovereignty for their own ends and with impunity. Like many Mozambicans, I lived through decades when South Africa did as it pleased in Mozambique in order to protect the interests of the apartheid regime. During this period many Mozambicans were killed or had their lives destroyed. It is to them that I dedicate this book.

Lília Momplé

Whoever does not know from where they come
Does not know where they are
Nor where they are going

19.00 HOURS

In the home of Narguiss

From the small verandah of her flat, Narguiss is once again contemplating the sky where, contrary to what the *moulanas* say must be, not even a trace of moon can be seen. It is a clear May sky dotted with stars of such intense brightness that they give the impression of being very close by. But Narguiss can see nothing of the moon and this makes her feel disappointed and uneasy.

'A people doesn't know what to do . . . To celebrate Eid without moon coming out, is not to be sinning?' she asks herself.

She continues to scrutinise the darkness as if waiting for an answer that will calm her anxiety. No sign comes from a sky that is withholding the moon, so she decides to begin her preparations for Eid. Her huge body sways as she walks towards the kitchen where she finds her youngest daughter already preparing samosas.

'Muntaz, my daughter; what a thing . . . To celebrate Eid with no moon coming out!' she complains, addressing herself to the girl whose beauty is enhanced in the soft luminous glow of the paraffin lamp.

'It will come out, Mother. It has already been seen in South Africa,' her daughter answers gently.

'But we is not at South Africa. So we be obliged to cook all night.'

'It's custom, Mother. The *moulanas* are the ones that know.'

'It's custom now. Before it never be custom to celebrate Eid without moon coming in the correct sky.'

Muntaz smiles and continues to prepare the filling for the

samosas, while watching her mother out of the corner of her eye with an expression at once ironic and tender.

As she goes to fetch the meat and other ingredients for the curry Narguiss tries not to bump against the stove, nor the table and the benches that clutter the kitchen. She is still mumbling under her breath about having to celebrate Eid without first seeing the new moon, even if it has appeared in the sky of South Africa. She cannot resign herself to such a practice. It goes against all her experience as a woman born, bred and raised in the bush, where the *moulanas* are guided only by their own eyes and not by news from neighbouring countries.

'We is not going to sleep tonight. We has to cook samosa, curry, *gilebe*, *mahaza*, all on a rush,' she laments.

'And Mother must be very happy to have so much to cook. Most of the people here have nothing. They celebrate with *ushua* and cabbage – nothing else,' responds Muntaz quietly.

'It's true . . . you is right, many doesn't have nothing,' agrees Narguiss after a brief silence, turning to her daughter indulgently, with a mixture of sweetness and stupidity.

'Especially the blacks, but also the *mestiços* like us. The pure Indians, they always find something,' adds Muntaz.

Narguiss agrees with her daughter again, while thanking Allah for her Abdul, son of a *cafusa* mother – a mixture of Indian and black – and an Indian father. Abdul takes completely after his father in his easy charm, a quality that has smoothed his path to prosperity, and for this reason Narguiss is immensely grateful to him.

It is, indeed, extraordinary that at a time of such extreme shortages, the woman's fridge does not want for goat meat, beef, large fish, butter and cool drinks. Nor is there any shortage of rice, sugar, flour, vermicelli or spices in the pantry. Everything is obtained through Abdul's 'schemes', into which she has never tried to delve. He has always supported the family in such a

4

way that they have never wanted for anything and were it not for the continuing problems with women, Narguiss would consider Abdul the perfect husband.

'Where is he your father now?' she asks aloud, following the thread of her own thoughts.

Muntaz does not answer, continuing to chop onions and chillies for the samosa filling.

'Where is he?' asks Narguiss again.

'Mother knows very well where he is,' says her daughter gently.

'With that woman . . . that Macua girl, that thief of husbands.'

And while she fills the mincing machine with small pieces of soft red meat, Narguiss does not tire of repeating how dangerous the women of the Island of Mozambique are, and how they like to steal the husbands of others.

Muntaz remains, as always, bemused by her mother's capacity to lie to herself about her husband's affairs; for her mother, it is always the women who pursue him until they catch him – *poor man* – 'in their clutching claws'.

She agrees, though, that her mother has a point in considering this particular Macua more dangerous. With other lovers, Abdul might sleep away from home on many consecutive nights, might walk out with the girls, might even put them up in a house and lavish them with gifts until his enthusiasm had passed. His passion was always violent and brief, like a tropical storm. But his liaison with the young Zena is different. It has now lasted for more than four years. Indeed, Abdul has found an opportunity to be with Zena most of the time. When Muntaz, his youngest daughter, announced that she wanted to go to Maputo to study at the country's only university Abdul said she could do so only if her mother accompanied her. Narguiss finally agreed to his plan and left the Island, taking her daughters with her. As soon as she departed, leaving Abdul on his own, he lost no time in bringing the little Macua beauty into his own house.

Through people who come from the Island, Muntaz hears how her father fawns upon the beautiful Zena. Some even say that Abdul has also taken his lover's youngest sister into the house to keep her company. And the most spiteful of all say that he sleeps with the two of them, and that they don't mind, because all they really wish from him is the easy, comfortable life that he provides for them.

For Muntaz, however, what is most alarming is that her father has not come to spend Eid with them. She knows that no matter how involved Abdul is with a woman, this day is always kept sacred for Narguiss and his three daughters. This time, though, he limited himself to a passing visit, staying only long enough to shop for the Feast. Soon afterwards, indifferent to his wife's pleading and the resentful silence of his daughters, he packed his suitcases and returned to the Island, promising to come back. But today is the eve of Eid and he has still not done so. And this sordid evasion deeply offends the sensitive Muntaz because, besides provoking great suffering in her mother, it covers the whole family with shame.

'Day of Eid to abandoning us here, without father, without husband,' sighs Narguiss, as if echoing her daughter's thoughts.

Muntaz remains silent, working the dough for the popadoms. Words of consolation seem meaningless at this moment, and she is relieved when her mother's attention turns to her two elder sisters who burst into the kitchen from the street.

'But . . . you doesn't be scared walking in the street at this time without light?' chides Narguiss.

The girls explain themselves, saying that the dressmaker has only just given them the clothes they are going to wear for the first time at Eid. Narguiss observes them tenderly, but not without a little anxiety. Actually she has been worrying about them for some time, worrying that neither Rábia nor Dinazarde, both now well into their twenties, has 'grabbed a husband'. This despite each being as desirable as a soft ripe fruit, with skin the colour of tea, shining black eyes, full breasts and well-shaped buttocks. To their mother's great despair men, attracted at first sight by the sensual, provocative beauty of the girls, invariably end up by turning away from their too overt charms.

Narguiss has already consulted the most famous *curandeiros* because the failure of Rábia and Dinazarde to marry can only be attributed to some very strong spell. The *curandeiros* all charge large sums for their prayers and drumming, all promise spectacular about-turns in the girls' fortunes, providing time-tables and everything necessary. 'By the end of this month a man with good position is going to appear . . . A week will not pass and a rich boy will . . .' But time passes and nothing happens. So Narguiss lives tormented by the fear of being ridiculed as the mother of three spinster daughters.

Not that the youngest daughter lacks suitors. But to the desolation of her mother, the girl doesn't even want to hear of marriage. She has always devoted herself to her studies, even though this has led to her whole family considering her unfemi-nine. Thus, when she completed her ninth year of school, Muntaz had to fight hard against her parents' opposition in order to study beyond the limits considered normal in their milieu. 'Study so much for what? Woman is not made to fill their heads with books,' they argued.

To persuade them to the contrary, and unable to use reason, the girl tried everything, from begging, to accusatory silence, to refusing to eat. Knowing how obstinate Muntaz could be, Narguiss and Abdul surrendered, hoping that later she would think about marriage and her role as a woman. They were not proud when she finished high school and wanted to study medicine in Maputo at the only university in the country. But by then Abdul was obsessed with the beautiful Zena and saw an opportunity for himself. Wishing to be free of his wife – at least for a while – Abdul, with apparent reluctance, had agreed that his daughter could study in the city, but only if Narguiss went with her.

And so it was that due to a father's amorous whim, Muntaz enrolled at the Faculty of Medicine. From the beginning she knew the value of hard work, and avoided everything that might distract her from realising her dream of becoming a doctor. Nonetheless, boys soon began to pay attention, and when they did, her mother tried to persuade her youngest daughter to accept those who seemed most suitable. But gradually Narguiss realised that nothing positive was achieved by her advice, the girl was determined to finish her course, and the older woman reluctantly left her Muntaz in peace.

Today, Narguiss is almost resigned to her daughter's extraordinary dedication to her studies at the expense of 'grabbing a husband'. But, if she reluctantly accepts this 'aberration', she does not feel the same about her two older daughters, who seem dogged by bad luck. In the feeble light of the paraffin lamp, she contemplates them tenderly and not without a little apprehension.

'Come, girls, go change clothes and come help. Everything are very late,' she says, following the two young women with her eyes. Observing them, blooming and perfumed like flowers, she is once again convinced that only a spell, a very strong spell, is keeping them single, year after year . . .

In the home of Leia and Januário

'It's good to be here . . . it's so good to be here,' says Leia to herself, revealing her immense capacity to live intensely, absorbing happiness from the smallest things, and finding advantage even in life's difficulties.

At first, the power cuts, which the city has been enduring for many months, left her disorientated and anxious. But little by little, she has learnt to live with this privation, just as she has become used to having only two dresses and never eating meat or fish – other than processed mackerel.

She has also learned to make the most of the time between her return from work and the hour at which the power cuts normally end, by playing with her two-year-old daughter, sitting in the only comfortable chair in the room, an old rocking chair bought second-hand. Here she allows herself a welcome break from her daily chores – the continuous moving around – at once so monotonous and so agitating as to seem devoid of meaning.

For this reason, at this moment, she is almost happy, softly rocking herself in the old chair and feeling on her skin May's fresh breeze that comes from the street, carrying the scent of red flamboyant flowers. With her daughter now asleep on her pregnant belly, she rejoices in the soft serenity of the night, which seems more enveloping in the absence of artificial light. She sits next to the door that opens onto the small balcony, which faces the street. And just as she has done on every other evening since they moved into the flat, Leia observes her room with deep pride. Standing against the far

9

wall, the small formica cupboard contains almost all the crockery she possesses. In the centre, a table and four chairs, also of formica, complete the furniture which, being so sparse and simple, makes the room seem open and spacious. The beautiful Mecufi grass mat that covers the floor, and her African violets in little pots in the corner, provide touches of refinement and freshness, as do the curtains whose poor quality Leia has tried to disguise with a cheerful finish of layered frills. She smiles at the memory of the hours stolen from her rest, as she worked on cutting them out and patiently tacking and sewing them at the house of her friend, Atalia, who has a sewing machine.

Leia loves these cheap curtains, the formica furniture, the plain glass crockery, the corner with its violets, the straw mat from Mecufi, the big rocking chair. For her all these things have an inestimable value because of the many sacrifices that went into acquiring them.

In addition to the living room, the flat has one small bedroom, a bathroom and a kitchen, both tiny, and a cubicle, which serves as a pantry. The living room is really the only one with standard dimensions but even so Leia marvels every day at the mere fact of having a home just for herself and her small family. Long before they married, she and Januário had presented all the necessary documentation to the State Administration for Immovable Property to enable them to rent a house or a flat, even one of the smallest. And then they subjected themselves to all the rigmarole required of them: meeting with requests for information, supplying certificates, making declarations, and applying for interviews that were endlessly postponed – the manager is in a meeting . . . only the manager can decide . . . come back next week . . . the house you went to see has already been let . . . we have a lot of people who applied before you . . . there is nothing available. . . .

Some people advised them to pay a bribe, but *only* a 'fat' one, they said. Januário could not agree to this, partly because it was against his principles and partly because he wouldn't have known where to find this kind of money anyway. So, eventually they gave up trying, got married and went to live with Leia's mother and sisters in Matola, as Januário had been sharing a room with a friend and Leia had been living in a residence run by nuns.

They used to leave from Matola at daybreak to travel to their work, braving the groups of armed bandits that daily infested that zone, robbing and murdering defenceless people. In order to arrive punctually, they had to spend almost everything they earned on the 'chapa cem' taxis, because the *machimbombos* followed an unpredictable timetable and, sometimes, without warning, would not appear for days.

The atmosphere in Leia's mother's house was similarly loaded with small irritations. These had accumulated to such an extent that they jeopardised the young couple's relationship. Januário, in particular, could not free himself of the feeling of being always in the way, which was not surprising since there was so little space. So that Januário could be alone with Leia in the room that she and her sisters had previously shared, the two younger sisters had had to drag their mattresses out into the living room, because there was not enough space to accommodate them in their mother's room. And sometimes the girls would grumble, even in front of Januário, as they improvised their beds on the floor. Then at dawn, when the boy had to tip-toe across the room to the bathroom to get dressed, they would glare at him suspiciously if they were awake, and hurriedly pull their sheets up to their chins.

Januário became deeply irritated with these and other attitudes held by his sisters-in-law, because he could not stand dubious or complicated relationships. His irritation, aggravated by lack of money, was reflected in the way he spoke and, at other times, in obstinate silences that stifled any dialogue. Sometimes, guiltily obeying a pang of conscience, because he knew that Leia was suffering from the situation as much as he was, he would cover her face with passionate kisses. But shortly afterwards he might again explode for some small reason and then spend entire days without speaking.

One day a friend of Leia's confided in her – but warning her to keep her secret very quiet – that the director-general of the ministry where she worked happened to be a big buddy of the director of the State Administration for Immovable Property and, therefore, an excellent benefactor – someone with the potential to solve Leia's housing problem.

Overcoming her natural timidity and an old reluctance to beg favours, Leia asked for an audience with the influential director-general. Even now, more than a year later, she still remembers that painful meeting with a shiver of indignation.

'Sit down,' said the director-general, without looking at her, when she entered his office.

Leia, well aware of her lowly position as a clerk, sat on the edge of one of the chairs arranged in front of a desk made of *jambire* wood.

'So, what's your problem?' the director-general finally asked, now smiling, and looking her up and down.

At that moment all Leia wanted was to run away from his penetrating eyes and his languid smile, so full of innuendo. To force herself to remain seated she had to think of Januário, and of the pleasant surprise she would give him if she succeeded in getting the director-general to intercede on their behalf, enabling them, finally, to rent a small apartment. Struggling to appear calm and serene, she began to report the anxiety she had gone through at the State Administration for Immovable Property; and how she had been told that he, the director-general, might be able to help her because he was such an influential person and . . . All the while she could feel that the man was examining her in minute detail, even with his eyes half closed, and that he was only listening with half an ear to what she was saying. She would not have been surprised if he had suddenly jumped on her like a tiger. But she remained glued to her chair, telling her story, while automatically pulling down her skirt, which had a tendency to rise, leaving a part of her thighs at the mercy of his greedy eyes. She was feeling really bad, all the more so because she was not used to being appreciated by men in such a shameless way.

Truly, Leia was far from being a woman who wanted to draw attention to herself. She possessed a quiet, slightly hidden beauty, very common amongst the women of the South, with skin that was a dusky black, and a face with thin eyebrows, large calm eyes and full lips. Her well-shaped thighs and buttocks were the only seductive elements about her otherwise delicate body. The only interest she normally awakened in men was the sort that arose after a certain time of companionship, more in response to her cheerful, attentive manner than her physical charm. So the obviously lustful stares of the director-general made her uneasy. And the silence that followed, after she had stopped speaking, served only to increase her embarrassment.

'I actually know the big shot at the State Administration for Immovable Property quite well,' said the director-general at last. 'He is my friend, so we'll solve your problem.'

Full of renewed hope, Leia felt that her efforts had not after all been wasted, sitting in his office and suffering his gaze. She was just about to thank him and leave when, with the gesture of someone who still has something important to say, the man continued calmly:

'You have your problem, but I also have mine. It seems that

we can help one another . . . I solve your problem and you solve mine, not so?'

'I don't understand,' stammered Leia to gain time, for she understood his veiled proposition only too well.

The director-general sat silent, as if giving her time to think. As she said nothing, he asked, in a voice now tinged with impatience, 'Well . . . are we in agreement?'

'Agreement . . . sincerely, I don't understand, Sir,' murmured Leia, still trying to tread water.

'Look . . . don't waste my time. What problem of mine could you solve? It can only be one, not so?'

For a moment, Leia was tempted to accede. She was so tired of trying to resolve a situation that had been dragging on for years and eating away at her life. She knew that some of her colleagues gave themselves regularly to any man who would give them money to feed their children. Why not her? To get a roof over her head, a place to live with her husband and her daughter? She had nothing to lose . . .

'So, why are you so silent?' the director-general asked, irritated.

Leia didn't know what to say, torn between her strong desire to rent a flat and her repulsion at the idea of giving herself to any man other than Januário. Besides, this man aroused in her a feeling of nausea.

The director-general misinterpreted her silence, stood up, and moved towards her. He slid his hand down her cleavage, grabbed her breast, and squeezed it with an insolent arrogance. Leia leapt up from her chair and ran out of the office. Everything happened very quickly and silently but now, more than a year later, she still remembers her last clear image of the director-general looking perplexed, his right hand in the air, tensed in the shape of a shell.

As if trying to brush this image out of her memory, Leia rocks

14

her chair to and fro more quickly. The movement wakes her daughter who begins to cry and call out for her father.

'Sleep, sleep, Daddy's coming soon,' Leia says gently, stroking her daughter who seems unusually agitated.

The child soon falls back to sleep, and Leia recovers the thread of her memories: the unsuccessful battles she fought to rent an apartment and how at last she succeeded by a stroke of luck. After the meeting with the director-general, she began to live with the permanent sensation of having played and lost her final card. In her mother's house there were moments when she felt as if she were suffocating – trapped between the insinuation of her sisters (what kind of man is this who cannot even rent you somewhere to live?) and the outbursts and silences of her husband. Not even the birth of little Iris succeeded in making the atmosphere any less tense. In a way, having another mouth to feed made things worse, with food only available on the black market or in the Interfranca foreign-exchange supermarket. There were times when Januário seemed to be in the mood to talk, when they both would try to find a solution, but they always concluded that, for the time being at least, they were in a dead-end street.

Then, suddenly, an answer arrived, at least for the short term. It took the form of one of Leia's childhood friends who had looked her up one day. She told Leia that her husband, lucky man, on first-name terms with various ministers, had won a bursary to study overseas for five years, with the right to take his family with him. So she proposed that during her absence, Leia and her husband live in their flat. She didn't want to give it up, foreseeing the difficulties that she would have in renting another one on their return. All in a fluster, Leia accepted the proposal immediately, agreeing to pay the rent on the apartment for five years and to bring her own furniture with her as her friend's had already been sold for a good price.

That night she and Januário could hardly sleep for the excitement of planning their new life. Then came the scurrying around to buy the bare minimum to furnish the flat – modest furniture, all second-hand – and counting every metical. And now Leia, her eyes accustomed to the darkness, never tires of contemplating the formica furniture, her African violets flowering in the corner, the Mecufi mat, the cheap curtains – everything that surrounds her – with the pride of someone who has fought hard to get what she has. Savouring the peace and silence of this perfumed May night, she repeats to herself:

'It is good to be here . . . How good it is to be here . . .'

In the home of Mena and Dupont

Romualdo, better known as Romu, slowly pours whisky into a glass, measuring it with his eyes. Putting the bottle on the table, he begins to sip his drink, holding the glass tightly in his fat hand.

'I don't know how you can drink it like that. At least some ice . . .' comments Dupont, the owner of the house.

'I like whisky straight . . . It's healthier that way,' counters the other, smacking his lips.

Of the three men in the room he seems to be the one in control. He even gives the impression of enjoying the situation. However, like the others, he wishes the hours would pass, that everything was over and that he had the agreed money in his pocket. He is a huge man, whose skin colour, an opaque black, scarcely allows the light of the paraffin lamps to reveal his features.

'Drink something too,' he says, his speech slightly slurred. 'It helps to pass the time.'

The others, understanding the hidden irony of the advice, don't respond.

'How I envy this guy,' thinks Dupont, observing the well-built man with a sudden resentment. 'He behaves as if he were the owner of the house and I his servant. Since he arrived he hasn't stopped giving orders. "Bring me whisky. Turn off the radio. The sound irritates me. Tell your wife to keep us company." But there is no doubt that the guy has balls. It's as if he were going out to a big party.'

As though reading his thoughts, Romu says suddenly:

'Are you nervous? Not me. It even reminds me of the good times we had in the army when we used to go and hunt *terrs*. You can't imagine the pleasure I felt when I sent someone to the other world. I only regret that I did this to so few . . . those guys were not easy to track down. Now the ones we are going to liquidate tonight are two little angels who already have their wings to fly to . . .'

He laughs at his own words while the others try vainly to accompany him.

'Come on. Drink up! It gives you courage,' he insists when he has stopped laughing.

'I don't like to drink when I work,' says Zalíua who has so far remained silent.

'A vice from your police days,' laughs the other. 'I'll have none of that, man. The head becomes lighter . . . But if none of you wants any, there'll be all the more for me.'

With his earlier solemnity, he pours himself a little more whisky, slowly sizing up the measure with his heavy-lidded eyes.

'And the lady of the house is not coming to keep us company . . . a little company?' he asks in a loud voice, so that he can be heard outside the room.

'My wife has better things to do,' replies Dupont, irritated. He is upset at the other's insistence on calling Mena into the room, the more so because he mistrusts his intentions.

'He's scared that I'll eat her pussy,' thinks Romu, laughing quietly to himself at his host's irritation. . . . 'It's true I could really eat her . . . a woman wasted on this chicken from Mauritius.'

'Besides, I don't want my wife to have anything to do with this business. She knows nothing about it,' continues Dupont.

'I think he's right. This is not a woman's business,' agrees Zalíua.

Romu doesn't respond, sipping his neat whisky and savouring every swallow as if it were his last.

Meanwhile, in the kitchen, Mena strains to hear what the three men are discussing, even though she has understood nothing of their scheming. But she has no doubt that the matter is very serious. She has had a sense of foreboding ever since these strange men began to appear in her house. And she doesn't know which of them frightens her more: the dark, strong one with the square, evil face and rough voice, or the other one – quiet, skinny, and with sharp, fleeting, snake-like glances.

Whenever she tries to find out from her husband what these men, who make him so agitated, are coming to do, he answers with the inevitable, 'Shut up! It's none of your business.' Nowadays it seems almost impossible for her to have any dialogue with Dupont. Sometimes she doubts that he considers her a human being: at least not one that thinks and feels like any other person. She wonders whether he just keeps her at home to do the housework, like a machine, and to be at his disposal to enjoy in his greedy, hurried way.

Dupont has no obvious vices and maintains her – this is the worst of it – because he considers himself a husband deserving of all her attention and all his rights, which includes beating her. The last time he did so was just three days ago; and it happened precisely because of the two men who are now sitting in the other room. . . . They had been talking with Dupont in low voices for many hours, and when they left, Mena noticed that her husband's hands were shaking and his behaviour betrayed extreme nervousness.

'I don't like the look of those men. I don't know why, but they scare me,' she commented at supper, observing her husband's hands, which where trembling so much they could hardly hold his knife and fork.

'Scare you?' asked Dupont, startled.

'Yes. And you become nervous whenever they show up. Look . . . your hands are shaking.'

'Shaking? Are you crazy?'

'Yes, they're shaking. I don't know why but I have a bad feeling about these men. There's something suspicious about them, and I can see that you don't want me to hear your conversations.'

'Shut up . . . Bloody hell, can't I invite and talk to whoever I want?' Dupont shouted.

'I just don't want you to get into trouble,' concluded Mena.

This was the final straw. The man had jumped up from his chair and slapped the woman twice, with a force that left her face burning for hours.

'I've already told you not to interfere in my life. You eat with my money, don't you? The rest is my business,' Dupont yelled.

From the intensity of his fury, Mena immediately understood that there was something about his relationship with the two men that really frightened him . . . and these two men were now in her living room.

For quite a while she has linked the two visitors with the appearance of foreign currency that her husband has been showing off lately. When, about two months ago, he began coming home with whisky, wine, meat, chicken, butter and other forgotten extravagances, she couldn't resist asking him how he had managed to obtain such luxuries from the Interfranca. Dupont, who always underestimated the reasoning power of women, especially his own, referred vaguely to 'business' and allowed no further discussion.

Despite her modest four years of schooling, Mena is far from stupid. She was not slow to realise that the 'business' could not be free of danger. On the day that Dupont slapped her, she became even more convinced of it. Finally, when her husband told her to prepare dinner for his two new friends, and also for the two foreigners, and warned her never to speak to anyone about their presence in his home, she was left with the certainty that something very serious was about to happen. And happen tonight. So now while she prepares the dinner in the kitchen, poorly lit by the paraffin lamp, she tries hard to understand what they are saying. But all she manages to hear is Romu's strong voice demanding her presence in the living room. For the rest she only catches isolated words which, dislocated from their context, remain meaningless.

'So is dinner on its way?' asks Dupont, bursting suddenly into the kitchen.

On hearing him, Mena jumps, smothering a scream with her hand. She has been so absorbed in her thoughts that she was unaware of her husband's approach.

'Don't be scared, it's only me,' says Dupont, looking very frightened himself.

'I'm scared all the time these days,' replies his wife.

'Don't start with your sarcasm. Is dinner coming or not?'

'It is,' she says dryly.

'Everything must run smoothly. These are posh people, white South Africans. So watch what you do.'

'South Africans?' asks Mena, feeling faint. 'But what have

white South Africans come to do in our house? You told me they were from Malawi.'

'Yes. They come from Malawi. Or, in other words, they came through Malawi ... but they are South Africans. Do you have a problem with that?'

'Those people just bring trouble. It's dangerous ... Now I understand why you don't want me to speak to anyone about them. They've come illegally, haven't they? Please don't ...'

'Shut up before I give you a beating right now,' interrupts Dupont, speaking into his wife's ear. 'A South African is like any other person. And don't make me nervous. Just take care of the dinner and shut up, otherwise I'll beat you black and blue right in front of these people.'

Mena falls silent, aware that there is no point arguing, no point to anything. A profound sense of hopelessness and an irrepressible desire to cry takes hold of her. To cry for something that is about to happen: but she doesn't know what, and it is this that makes it even more terrifying. Mechanically she continues to prepare the dinner; and mechanically, when everything is ready, she takes the tablecloth and serviettes through to the living room.

Romu welcomes her with an exuberant show of appreciation but, in the face of her heavy silence and her husband's severe frown, he leaves his loud compliments hanging in the air. Nevertheless, nothing can prevent him from admiring the mature beauty of the woman who in the light of the paraffin lamp has acquired an air of mystery.

He observes her while she moves from one side to the other, laying the cutlery and plates on the table which, little by little, takes on an almost festive appearance. Whenever possible he sneaks a furtive look at her strong, well-shaped legs. He is fascinated by the woman's supple waist, but what really turns him on is her full mouth, with its well-defined upper lip, and her

21

languid dark eyes, in the depths of which he senses a permanent sexual frustration.

'If I could catch you, I'd show you what a real man is,' he thinks. 'What a waste of a woman in the hands of this Mauritian weakling! The guy is so nervous that he's jumping up and down like a locust . . . And a woman like that in the hands of such shit.'

To console himself against such injustice Romu pours himself a little more whisky, slamming the half-empty bottle down on the table. Dupont, meanwhile, doesn't let him out of his sight. He suspects that Romu has been desiring his wife since the first day he set foot in the house. Such insolence hurts him doubly. The mere fact that somebody desires his wife is enough to arouse his possessive instincts, but that this person also happens to be black, a kaffir, triggers his deep-seated racism. So he doesn't take his eyes off Romu, as if he fears that the man will suddenly lay his paws on the woman.

Mena, since entering the room, feels as if she is being undressed, but she doesn't know whose gaze is heavier with lasciviousness – Romu's, openly insolent, or Zalíua's, fleeting and sharp like a snake. In silence, she finishes laying the table and goes to empty the ashtray, now full of Zalíua's butts. When she returns with the clean ashtray, Romu invites her to sit down, his smile revealing his strong white teeth. Zalíua, in turn, peers at her slyly.

'No . . . no. My wife has much to do in there. Go . . . go and finish preparing the food,' Dupont says quickly.

Mena leaves without hesitation. It was not her intention to remain in a room where the presence of three such men is suffocating.

21.00 HOURS

In the home of Narguiss

The power cut has ended and the small kitchen in which Narguiss and her youngest daughter are still busy with preparations for Eid is now well lit. Due to the lack of space, Rábia and Dinazarde are working in the adjacent pantry – not that this has prevented them from joining in the conversation.

'Go and see who it is!' shouts Narguiss suddenly.

Somebody has rung the doorbell and, hearing it, Narguiss feels her heart leap in her big chest, full of hope that it may finally be Abdul. Besides, she has always expected her husband to come and spend Eid with his family, and so the late hour does not surprise her, given the complete unreliability of flights from the North.

Hearing the agitated tones of her mother's voice, Muntaz senses what she is feeling and experiences a wave of compassion for this fat woman of such generous stupidity, with such a predisposition to forgive: a compassion that suffocates her when, instead of her father's voice, she hears the raucous greetings of her cousin Fauzia.

'Ah . . . it's Fauzia,' says Narguiss, in a flat voice, returning painfully to reality.

Meanwhile their guest has entered the kitchen and, after asking after the health of her cousins, provides them with details of her own minor ailments, while apologising for having arrived so late . . . but Eid, this year – nobody understands why – the moon doesn't appear at the same time everywhere . . . and she has to see to her clothes, which are not yet ready, and still get the seasonings which are so difficult to find and . . .

She pauses suddenly, noticing her cousin's sad expression. 'Are you sick, cousin Narguiss?'

'No . . . it's nothing. I's just tired,' Narguiss replies hurriedly. Fauzia realises that something is wrong but, egocentric by nature, she soon forgets the look on her cousin's face and sits herself down in the pantry to chat with Rábia and Dinazarde.

Fauzia is in her late thirties; her face, still fresh, with surprisingly innocent eyes, is framed by beautiful black hair, which seems almost not to belong to her ballooning body. Youngest daughter of Narguiss' cousin, she has lived in the flat next door ever since she arrived in Maputo six years ago with her husband and her two sons. It was through her that Narguiss was able to rent the apartment in which she now lives.

'Have you realised that this is my last Eid in Mozambique?' boasts Fauzia, beginning to empty the enormous straw basket she has brought with her, because being family, she participates every year in the preparations for Eid with her cousins.

'You're still very determined,' says Muntaz ironically, from the kitchen.

'We'll manage to find something. Aren't my sisters doing well? And my brother-in-law, Momade, is going to find a job for Saleem and . . .'

'You know very well that your husband wants nothing to do with Momade. You yourself said . . .'

'That doesn't matter to me,' interrupts Fauzia, suddenly beside herself with irritation. 'We'll manage to find something. And I'm telling you once more, I would rather go begging in Portugal than live here.'

'It's no use speaking to you . . .' laments Muntaz.

'You're right, it's useless. I don't even know why you bother . . . Do you mean to frighten me?' replies the visitor, pointedly changing the subject.

Daughter of mestiço Indians, Fauzia belongs to that group of Mozambicans who were caught unprepared by the country's independence. Perfectly adapted to her condition as colonised with certain privileges, she found the idea of a fatherland too large to assimilate within her narrow horizons, where there is room for only a small circle of relatives and friends. And when these began to flee, a frenetic anxiety to leave took hold of her as well. Had it not been for her husband, who had held back her escapist impulses, she would long ago have settled in Portugal. But because of the sudden vacuum left by the settlers, Saleem came to hold a higher position in the bank in which he worked, and did not wish – at least right away – to abandon his new, comfortable situation in favour of vague promises of a job in an unknown country.

Not even the euphoric though badly written letters from Fauzia's sisters had encouraged him to leave Mozambique. For a while he suspected his sisters-in-law of lying, because he knew of several people who already regretted having left. However, his suspicions were unfounded, as he realised immediately when, for the first time, he went on holiday to Portugal.

His youngest sister-in-law, in particular, was constantly blessing the day her husband had decided to leave with their family for Lisbon. During all his life in Mossuril, he had never been more than an obscure shopkeeper, barely earning enough to eat, while in Portugal he had managed to amass a true fortune, by means of an audacity that could never have been foreseen.

Soon after arriving in the Portuguese capital with no job and no money, he joined a group of Ishmaelites like himself, who made their living by cheating the most ignorant and insecure 'returnees', extorting from them part of the money they received from the Institute for Assistance for Returnees from the Ex-colonies while at the same time also cheating IARNE itself.

Indeed, even today, the group is still involved in huge drug deals, and Fauzia's brother-in-law has been revealed as one of the most astute dealers. In this way he has managed to raise capital which, in a short time, has allowed him to become the owner of several residences, boarding houses and hotels, whose network expands as far as the Algarve. Among his most intimate friends, he boasts about the millions he has in various European banks, and of having bribed many people, including a Portuguese judge who has since become his accomplice. As for Fauzia's sister, indifferent to the way in which her husband has acquired his fabulous riches, she now lives in a permanent state of exhilaration, drunk on the luxury and comfort and the uncritical acceptance within society which wealth has bestowed on her. Fauzia's husband has witnessed all this.

His other sister-in-law, a divorced mother of eight, found a different way of surviving in Portugal. By crying, begging and exhibiting her litter of children, she managed to get certain institutes to help her with subsidies, rations and rent for her accommodation as a returnee. Not content with all this, she then set up a showy fortune-telling business in one of the rooms of her flat, replete with billowing cloths, where gullible people came to seek her out.

During her sessions, Fauzia's sister speaks in Macua because of her limited knowledge of Portuguese, with her eldest daughter acting as an interpreter. This has a marked effect on her European clients who are pleasantly impressed by the strange idiom of the language. So the self-styled fortune-teller has her hands full from morning till night attending to worried people, from simple saleswomen who leave most of their hard-earned savings in her hands, to the arrogant wives of ministers or the ostentatious and no less arrogant mistresses of those same ministers.

If ever someone who once knew her as a quiet housewife in Mozambique shows surprise at her new and unexpected occupation, Fauzia's sister just laughs and says that, had she known before what she knows now, she would have taken up fortune-telling a long time before, as it has provided her with an easy life. A fact that Fauzia's husband can vouch for.

Even so, his decision to leave for Portugal was not easy. Not that he was held back by feelings of patriotism or by scruples about using whatever illegal means he needed in order to succeed – but Saleem was afraid of exchanging an enviable financial situation for an adventure of uncertain outcome. Also he had never liked the idea of being employed by Momade, the husband of his eldest sister-in-law, who after becoming very rich, turned into a hard taskmaster with all his staff, including his relatives.

As time passed, however, and Fauzia did nothing but complain, life grew more and more difficult for her husband. At one stage Fauzia even threatened to leave for Portugal on her own, taking their children with her. She claimed they would be well received by her sisters, who were rich and didn't have chickens for husbands. At that point the man, who had a passionate affection for his two children – his eldest son having died at the age of five – became afraid that his wife would carry out her threats. He resolved, very much against his will, to abandon his country.

Fauzia considers it a great victory to have persuaded her husband to leave. So when Muntaz alludes to the risks of such a decision, Fauzia becomes very bad-tempered. It can only be jealousy, she thinks sourly. Anyway, she has never felt much affection for Muntaz, who seems to her to be almost abnormal in her mania for studying; and is so different from her sisters, who are normal girls, who like beautiful dresses and enjoying themselves, as is suitable for women their age.

Simmering with indignation, Fauzia leaves the apartment for a few minutes to go and fetch the spices that she has left at home. Making the most of the young woman's absence, Narguiss turns to Muntaz:

29

'Don't make fight with Fauzia, girl. Leave her, the heart of her says go to Lisbon, let her go . . .'

'She has no shame,' Muntaz says acerbically. 'So much big talk about her brother-in-law and her sisters and in the end they are just thieves.'

'Thieves?!' says Dinazarde, surprised.

'Yes, thieves. There are many ways of stealing. They don't go around assaulting people and breaking into houses, but they are thieves all the same. And Momade, besides being a thief is a murderer, because he sells drugs. They say he even sells them to schoolchildren.'

'But they also say he gives a lot of money to the poor,' interjects Rábia.

'Must be because he's scared of going to hell. Anyway, it's easy to give away stolen money,' says Muntaz cynically.

'Everyone tries to cope with their life. It's not their fault that others are dumb. I don't think they are thieves,' defends Dinazarde.

'Neither do I,' agrees Rábia. 'If I find a rich husband I won't give a damn how he gets his money.'

'That's why you can't find one,' replies Muntaz wickedly.

'Girls, stop these talkings. Everyone makes life like they can. We don't have nothing to do with that,' intervenes Narguiss, trying to end the discussion.

Secretly, she also disapproves of the subtle thoughts of her youngest daughter, which lead her to think that Fauzia's brother-in-law and sisters might really be thieves. And she is upset that her daughter is arguing so aggressively about a topic that does not really affect them. What, in her opinion, should concern them is that her eldest daughter cannot 'catch a husband', that they are having to celebrate Eid 'without moon coming out', and that Abdul is absent.

Abdul. Abdul. As the hours pass, the certainty that he will

30

not come to join the celebration with his family becomes increasingly painful, and Narguiss grows silent and distant, absorbed by the pain that slowly overcomes her. For the first time in so many years of marriage, she is scared of losing her husband forever. Scared because though innumerable women have passed through his hands, none has been able to keep him on such a sacred day. Only this one, this Macua, there on the Island, who according to what she has heard, reigns in her house and sleeps in her bed.

She begins to sigh. Listening to her mother's subconscious cries escaping from her poorly treated heart, Muntaz can hardly resist the impulse to throw her arms around this large woman to console her as she might a credulous, disoriented child. She stays where she is, though, looking at her mother out of the corner of her eye and cursing her father for making the older woman suffer so much. In the pantry, Fauzia and her cousins stop chattering, troubled by the strange wordless lament.

And for a few moments, in the sudden silence that falls over the five women, only the work of their knives, skimming ladles and wooden spoons accompany the long heart-wrenching sighs of unspoken pain.

In the home of Leia and Januário

Leia watches her husband. He eats the reheated *ushua* and cabbage, which she has brought in from the kitchen, in silence. They are seated at the table in the living room. Januário has just arrived from night school where he is a teacher, and he savours the bland dinner with obvious satisfaction. Seeing him eat with such pleasure, a wave of gratitude washes over Leia. She knows her husband appreciates how difficult it is to prepare meals without the wherewithal to make them tasty.

In fact the only products available in the Maputo market over the last three years have been maize meal, cabbage and, sometimes, frozen mackerel. As for the rest, either it doesn't exist or it is sold on the black market, and at the Interfranca to *co-operantes* and the few Mozambicans with privileged lifestyles, or falls into the hands of thieves. The ordinary worker has had to make do with *ushua* and cabbage which, in popular parlance, has become known as 'if it weren't for you'.

Leia can no longer stand cabbage, especially at dinner; she prefers dry bread and tea, even without sugar, which is also rare. That is why it is always with surprise and delight that she observes her husband's calm movements as he lifts large forkfuls of food to his mouth, and chews them with pleasure. She is perpetually grateful to him for not being like so many other men who, especially on Sundays, fill the restaurants, where they consume their entire salaries in one plate of meat or fresh fish, leaving the *ushua* and cabbage at home for their wives and children. The pride she feels in knowing that she is respected, is reflected in the smile which at this moment lights up her face and which her husband notices between two mouthfuls.

'You are happy today! Your day went well, no?' he comments in his abrupt, decisive way.

'It's not that,' answers Leia, smiling. 'I'm always surprised to see you eating with such an appetite, especially as it is always the same thing. It's good to be like you.'

'What else can we do? It's what we have. And you, didn't you eat? Or was it just bread with tea?'

'You guessed . . . Sometimes just the smell of cabbage makes my stomach turn.'

Januário abstains from comment because he understands that

his wife has had more than enough of this monotonous menu, one that she is obliged to prepare every day.

'Perhaps it is because you've been through so much . . .' says Leia, picking up the conversation.

'Perhaps,' says Januário, still chewing, while exchanging a look of understanding with his wife.

He knows how shocked Leia was when, some time after they had met, he had told her about his life, which had already been filled with sorrow. And he knows that even though she avoids talking about the events that caused his suffering, she keeps them safe in her heart.

Januário was born in a village lost among the forests of Alto Molocue, which had been utterly destroyed by Renamo. It lay in such a remote spot that only when all the *curandeiro*'s remedies had been exhausted would a villager venture as far as the nearest health post. Where school was concerned, no one had any memory of any of its inhabitants ever having frequented such a place.

Fear, without a doubt, was the feeling that dominated the first years of Januário's life. Fear of the wild animals that forced the villagers to lock themselves in their huts before sunset, as during the night they circled the village, filling the air with their haunting cries. Fear also of the devastating storms which the surrounding forest attracted. And, as he got older, fear of the white man – specifically the head of the local administrative post, a mythical, inaccessible character, whose presence was only felt through his terrifying black sepoys.

Actually the very remoteness of the village protected it from the assaults of the staff at the administrative post. Nevertheless, on the rare occasions that they did appear, they would always leave a trail of destruction, forcefully taking cattle, chickens, eggs, men for forced labour on the plantations, and sometimes even the most beautiful girls. His own father was twice taken for forced labour and, even today, Januário has a distinct memory of him disappearing around a bend in the path, between two sepoys, his head bowed, uncomplaining.

From a very young age, Januário was aware of the extreme poverty of the people in the village and, particularly, of his own family, whose work in the fields seemed only to generate want. His father was a man who, even by the time Januário was born, seemed to live in a state of permanent withdrawal from the world. Holding the ancestors in great esteem, his main pre-occupation was the meticulous performance of rituals for the dead: he barely seemed to notice the day-to-day misery of life around him. Januário's mother, on the other hand, who looked more like her husband's daughter than his wife, was a woman whose focus was on life and living: she was able to rejoice in the simple singing of birds or the clarity of the air after a storm. She was also, in her way, a fighter – even though she had shown this spirit on one occasion only. This was when Januário was fourteen years old and she had convinced him, against her husband's wishes, to leave for Nampula in search of work. His father wanted his son to become a peasant farmer like himself and his father and his father's father before him. But his mother wanted another destiny, whatever it might be, for her only remaining son (all the others had died while still children), because anything seemed better than being tied to the capricious earth, so vulnerable to storms that could raze the work of several months in just a few hours. Besides, the idea of one day seeing her son taken for *chibalo* frightened her.

She was full of apprehension as she watched Januário growing up because she knew that her husband did not share her ideas. But she also knew how to wait patiently. One day, taking advantage of a time when her husband was absorbed in the annual ceremonies held in honour of the ancestors, she convinced her son to join a group of young people who were leaving for Nampula. With pain in her soul, but with dry eyes, she prepared a small food parcel for him and gave him all her small savings accrued over years. The boy was far away by the time his father noticed his absence. The discussion with his wife was brief, as she had expected, for it was difficult for him to worry simultaneously both about the annual ceremonies and the absence of his son.

'He knows he's our only son and he will return to bury us,' Januário's mother said finally. In these words her husband found comfort.

Meanwhile, Januário and his new companions – five youngsters in all – supported each other on the long and dangerous journey to Nampula. They travelled on foot, along the dusty road, sometimes lined with such dense bush that even during the day, they could feel the gaze of wild animals watching them with hostile eyes. At sunset they sought shelter wherever they could find it and were invariably offered something to eat and a corner to sleep in. At dawn they took to the road again. They travelled in this manner all the way to Nampula. Even now, when Januário thinks about that first, unforgettable trip, he remembers with amazing clarity the infinite succession of green tones, the penetrating taste of dust, the scorching heat and the humid smell of the bush at twilight.

When they arrived in Nampula they all stayed with one of the young men's distant relatives and then they separated as they found work. As illiterate peasants, the only kind of work available to them was domestic work, which at least guaranteed them a roof over their heads, and food.

Januário went knocking on several doors before he found a place where, from the first moment, his instinct advised him to stay. He immediately liked the lady of the house, a mulatto woman with kind eyes and a smiling face, who offered to pay him well. At lunchtime he met her husband, who worked on the railways, and her grandchildren, a girl in her early teens with a beautiful face and petulant expression, and a little boy with disinterested eyes. They lived with their grandparents because in the village where their parents had a shop, there was no school.

The children and the man of the house did not seem to notice Januário's presence except to give him orders. But the lady, whose name was Florinda, gave him an almost maternal attention, concerning herself with feeding him and even with his comfort. The truth is that, especially at night, Januário was homesick for his parents and his village far away in the forest. At such times, even the howls of the wild animals circling the huts seemed to him like familiar music. Nevertheless, despite the sorrow of absence, he had no regrets about having come to Nampula.

Meanwhile, he tried hard to perfect himself in his work, partly out of fear of losing his job and partly to please Dona Florinda, towards whom his strong feeling of gratitude came soon to be mixed with pity, when he realised that this smiling lady was in fact far from happy.

The grandchildren, spoilt rotten, caused her to live in a state of constant anxiety. They demanded delicacies, which they then left on their plates, complaining that they could not eat them. They harassed her with endless requests for money for sweets and games, forcing her to subtract it from the meagre amount she had at her disposal to manage the house.

Her husband, who prayed with his rosary in the backyard every night, nonetheless neighed like a horny stallion whenever he saw a woman to whom he felt attracted. Even his two sisters-in-law did not escape his harassment. Thus, throughout her married life, Dona Florinda suffered shame – shame that few women would endure without looking for a way to retaliate. And, just three days before her husband suddenly died, he made her suffer one final humiliation. On that afternoon Dona Florinda was going to the hospital to visit a sick friend and, taking a short cut, decided to cross a piece of fallow land. As she approached an enormous baobab tree, she noticed a group of people observing with great intensity something that was moving near the tree's trunk. Some were laughing while others turned their backs in obvious indignation. Dona Florinda had hardly time to wonder what they had found to interest them, when she was suddenly confronted by her husband, who with glassy eyes and a flushed face was pulling up his zip. Next to him, a young woman with broad hips straightened her *capulanas* and, picking up an old basket, turned to leave. Dona Florinda's husband slipped off in the opposite direction, his head down.

'But this man has no shame,' an aged man commented in Macua, half offended, half joking.

'Shut up! That woman is his wife,' warned another man, also in Macua, pointing with his chin at Dona Florinda.

She understood the exchange, and the fact that she had been recognised did not surprise her. She and her husband had lived in Nampula for so many years that they were part of the town's human landscape. This was another reason why the pornographic achievements of her husband had always so humiliated her. And here she was again, standing as if fixed to the ground, listening to the laughing comments of the people dispersing.

Faint with shame, she gave up on the idea of going to the hospital. Instead, demanding of her shaking legs an extreme effort, she returned home with a feeling of profound disgust for her husband – a disgust which, strangely, embraced her as well. She did not know then that this would be the last time that this man, her husband, would humiliate her and that three days later, seated on a park bench, he would encounter death.

The poor relationship between the couple had been obvious

to Januário from the first day he began working in their house. With his growing understanding of Portuguese, he became better able to appeciate the full extent of Dona Florinda's suffering, both through her arguments with her husband and through the complaints she voiced to her most intimate friends.

Almost without realising it, the young man tried to ease Dona Florinda's pain, by doing his job with such dedication that she could not but appreciate it. And thus were planted the seeds, between employer and employee, of a growing feeling of mutual consideration, something that later allowed Januário to change the direction of his life. When, encouraged by the example of other young black men, he decided to study at night, he had Dona Florinda's unhesitating support. Her husband, in contrast, did not miss an opportunity to mock:

'So, you also want a degree. Don't you know that blacks can't have degrees? They have heads like monkeys.'

The grandchildren laughed at such mockery but Dona Florinda did everything she could to encourage Januário to study. Sometimes he listened to her commenting to her friends:

'Januário is so keen to study. On Sundays he doesn't even go out, he is glued to his books.'

'Better watch that he doesn't forget to do his work. I've never liked servants that study. They think they can be like the white man and don't want to work,' her friends would invariably retaliate.

'But this one goes on working even better than before,' Dona Florinda would reply defensively, never imagining how far these words would come to work in her favour.

For Januário, on hearing these exchanges, would try even harder to earn Dona Florinda's trust and to work to the best of his ability. He became truly indispensable to her to the point where she wondered how she had ever managed to live without the help of this useful, silent young man.

So Januário's life passed – the days framed by his job and his studies – without great expectations but also without great worries. This was until the day that the Bishop of Nampula, Dom Manuel Vieira Pinto, was expelled from the town.

From way back Januário had known that a war was spreading throughout the colony. Some of his colleagues had also told him of a nationalist movement called Frelimo, which was fighting in the bush. And even the military pomp displayed by the town of Nampula, the soldiers and military vehicles moving around at all hours, could only be understood as the rearguard action of a war in progress. It was, however, on that memorable day, when a number of enraged whites forced the expulsion of another white of such importance as the Bishop of Nampula, that Januário first perceived that something irreversible was about to happen in his country.

On that day, frightened by the news that had been circulating throughout the town from early morning, Dona Florinda advised him not to leave the house for any reason. Groups of white men, in cars and on foot, were shouting on the streets, demanding the expulsion of Dom Manuel, and venting their anger by beating every black they encountered. They also demanded that all public offices, restaurants and cafés close their doors until the bishop had left Nampula. Anyone who delayed fulfilling such orders would have their windows and furniture broken, without the police intervening to restrain this destructive euphoria.

True pandemonium broke out in the town, reaching a climax when a multitude of yelling whites gathered in front of the bishop's residence. At the tops of their voices, they demanded the expulsion of Dom Manuel, while simultaneously waving insulting banners and placards on which the face of the prelate was drawn with the enormous ears of a donkey.

Calm only returned in the middle of the afternoon when the

bishop, confronting the now hoarse mob, silenced it with the simple strength of his long, quiet gaze. Then, with a calm serenity that paralysed even the most enraged, he walked to his car, which was already waiting to take him to the airport from where he would fly to Lourenço Marques. There his destiny would be decided.

Januário came to know of these happenings through his colleagues at night school, some of whom had been victims of the beatings. He also came to know that the reason for such hostility towards the bishop was a certain pastoral letter entitled 'Rethinking the War', which had been read out in all the Catholic churches in the diocese of Nampula. According to his friends, in the pastoral letter Dom Manuel stated: 'The war against the Mozambicans, who want only to be masters of their own land, is nothing but an unjust and cruel war.' Such brave words could not but provoke scandal and great animosity among the majority of the settlers.

For Januário, the fact that a white man, of such importance as the Bishop of Nampula, had been expelled by whites, because he had stood up for the blacks, was a sure sign of something new in the world in which he was living. This provoked in him feelings of fear and intense joy, much as was the case with the other blacks with whom he exchanged ideas and experiences. Meanwhile, in the house of Dona Florinda, people's conversations and attitudes showed only fear and insecurity, which were further exacerbated by the deposition of Caetano in Portugal and the overthrow of the fascist regime.

Even now, remembering the period between the coup d'état in Portugal and the day of Mozambique's independence, precisely fourteen months later, Januário has the impression that time was simultaneously advancing and receding. There was a succession of popular demonstrations, instructional meetings, the creation of new services and the ending of others, all in the midst of a contagious euphoria that was affecting most people. On the other hand, in certain circles of the town, a silent, expectant, almost tangible despair seemed to paralyse time.

Shortly before the great day of Mozambican independence, the flight of the discontented began. Entire families crowded onto aeroplanes, which were unable to cope with the demand. The less frightened were able to fill containers with everything they could carry. Others – fearing carnage, a bloodbath and other terrible events – fled, with only the basics, to face an unknown future in Portugal or in South Africa.

In Dona Florinda's house, the first to leave were her grandchildren. One day their parents arrived from the bush where they had abandoned their house and shop and, in a feverish fluster, organised the trip and left with their children. Dona Florinda and her husband kept finding reasons to delay their own departure, torn between a deep love for their land and the fear of living far away from their whole family who had left already. Januário was moved by the suffering of Dona Florinda, who was going to Portugal 'because it had to be', and who spent her days crying in the house that daily felt more empty without the children and their possessions.

Dona Florinda's husband, despite his continuing prayers with his rosary every night in the backyard, became as irascible as a rhinoceros. He hardly ate and never opened his mouth except to shout, which left him completely hoarse by the end of the day. Januário was the favourite target of his ire. His eyes held daggers every time he gave the young man an order, or he proceeded to abuse him as a 'shit Frelimo terrorist', in a tone full of ironic hatred. The young man endured these provocations with extreme patience, bearing in mind that Dona Florinda had asked him not to pay attention to her husband's words because he was disoriented. And truly the older man seemed disoriented, wandering around every day through the streets and gardens of the city

41

in a kind of pilgrimage, as if he wanted to remember everything that he would soon have to leave behind, for they had eventually decided that they would have to go.

A few weeks before the scheduled date of their departure, he left the house, as always, for a walk in the clear morning air, now perfumed by the mango trees in full bloom. He went to the park where he sat on his favourite bench, contemplating, already with longing, everything around him. It was there that they found him, around midday, already cold, his eyes wide open and with such a painful expression on his face that no one could say he had achieved peace in death. His love for his land had won; his body had refused to leave it.

Forgetting all his injustice, Dona Florinda wept sincerely for her husband and relied heavily on Januário's support throughout the burial ceremony. The young man's dedication was well rewarded because during the time remaining before her departure for Portugal, Dona Florinda did not rest until she had found him a job. She finally succeeded with the firm João Ferreira dos Santos.

By that time Januário had already completed standard four and, even if the salary he was earning at the firm was quite modest, that he was no longer working as a domestic servant proved a real incentive. Meanwhile he continued to study at night, despite his new job, although this left him mentally exhausted by the end of the day.

When, at last, she said goodbye to Januário, Dona Florinda was in tears. She gave him some money, which to him was a small fortune and which, some months later, allowed him to go home and visit his parents. That, as it turned out, was to be his first and only visit. A few years later, he received the news that they were dead, burned alive by armed bandits.

They had arrived at dawn, he was told, in Macua, by the bearer of these tidings, his father's youngest brother, Assane.

They were many and they were very young boys – almost children – all with guns.

Assane then told the terrible tale: how he had been surprised while asleep, by a group of five of these young men who had invaded his hut, their guns pointed at him and his trembling wife. With eyes bloodshot from smoking *suruma*, the boys spoke among themselves in Ndau. Assane, waiting passively for the shots that would surely carry them from this life, was greatly relieved when they ordered him and his wife to get out. The boys then laid waste their meagre belongings and set fire to their hut, the flames merging with those of the other burning huts. The air was filled with billowing smoke and unbearable cries.

The assailants operated in small groups. They entered huts, plundered them and then set them alight. They ordered the teenagers, young men and women out. The older people, small children and pregnant women were burned alive inside their own huts. If they tried to escape they were hunted down and killed – either shot or bayonetted. Januário's parents, whose hut was next to Assane's, were burned alive. Their screams still reverberate in Assane's ears.

Assane also described how, having burnt down all the huts in the village, the armed men forced the survivors to carry the products of their plunder on a long, painful march through the forest. Anyone who tried to run away was caught and beaten; those who collapsed from exhaustion or hunger were immediately shot. Such was the fate of Assane's wife who, having for three days carried on her head a sack of maize meal heavier than herself, eventually sank to the ground.

She made no effort to get up and the resigned smile with which she accepted death showed that it came to her as a relief. Assane had to witness the murder of his wife without being able to make the slightest movement. And, like all the others who had been shot, she was left without a grave, abandoned in the bush to the mercy of hyenas and vultures.

Summoning up his last ounce of will-power, Assane continued the march, struggling to keep up with the rhythm of the young armed men who, galvanised by *suruma*, showed no sign of weariness. The opportunity to escape arose when they were surprised by a platoon of the Armed Forces of Mozambique. Taking advantage of the subsequent confusion, Assane abandoned his load and ran, fearful and without direction, for several hours until he stopped and tried to reorientate himself. And, then, since his village did not exist any more, he decided to take the direction of Nampula in order to tell Januário about the death of his parents, and to look for refuge and for work. Once in the city, he slept for several days on a park bench and ate whatever people gave him. Eventually, by chance, he found a person from his home town, who despite not remembering him well, gave him shelter, found out – through his contacts – where Januário lived and took him to his nephew.

Januário, now an orphan, listened to what his uncle was telling him, without showing any emotion and without moving. Indeed, Assane sometimes doubted that his nephew was even listening to him, as he slowly made his troubled way through his story, the long pauses reflecting the effort it took to relate this macabre narrative. Januário remained silent, no matter how long Assane paused; the young man was wholly unprepared to assimilate the news he was receiving. Given the great difficulties of communication in a country so devastated by war, he was not even aware that his village had been attacked, even though such massacres had been a daily topic of conversation for a long while. But discovering, so suddenly, that his parents and his village no longer existed, he found himself bereft of speech. When, at last, he was able to react, he only asked in his home language:

44

'You mean to tell me that nothing . . . nothing exists any more?'

'Everything, everything was burnt to ashes,' confirmed his uncle, whose face had aged with pain.

Januário had never been an especially happy person, not even as a child, and from that day he grew still more silent and introverted. He began, too, to suffer from sudden intense headaches that descended on him for no apparent reason; and a chronic sense of anxiety prevented him from feeling well anywhere. So when, some time later, his firm transferred him to Maputo, he accepted the change with satisfaction.

Here he met Leia and, little by little, came to realise that her presence made him feel peaceful. When he finally realised that he could no longer live without her, he asked her to marry him. Without hesitation she accepted the almost ugly young man, with prominent cheekbones and a sad gaze, but in whose presence she felt a security she had felt with no other man. Januário then told her his life story, and so now Leia understands when he says:

'Yes, perhaps . . . perhaps it's because I have been through so much, that I can eat cabbage every day.'

In the home of Mena and Dupont

'Please stop that!' explodes Romu to the owner of the house who, with increasing frequency, stands up from his chair only to sit down again.

'Always up and down. Relax, dammit, the South Africans will come.'

'Leave me alone!' replies Dupont, 'I'm in my own house . . . I'll stand and sit as much as I want.'

'OK . . . OK,' says Romu, ironically conciliatory.

'Hey man, calm down, man,' intervenes Zalíua, who is chain-smoking. 'Dammit! What's needed now is a cool head . . .'

At this moment he seems to be the calmest of the three. As time passes and the effects of the whisky become stronger, Romu is becoming increasingly anxious. Besides, the almost constant movement of the owner of the house makes him all the more nervous.

'The time has already passed when they were supposed to arrive, and still nothing of those guys,' sighs Dupont, getting up and then sitting down again.

'They will come,' mumbles Zalíua, savagely stubbing the end of his cigarette in the ashtray, already full of butts.

'Of course they will come . . . and if they arrive late, there's no problem . . . everything is already prepared. Only the final details are missing,' jokes Romu, bursting into laughter – the nervous quality of which does not escape the other two.

An oppressive silence descends over the three, who look askance at each other, a silence that Mena feels in the kitchen and that perturbs her more than the occasional words she hears and whose meaning escapes her, detached as they are from their context.

She is seated on a bench trying to catch any possible sound that might break the ominous silence. She tries to think about something else, but cannot get the men in the living room out of her mind, and desperately asks herself what interests and anxieties might unite them and turn them into accomplices. She is ignorant of the fact that nothing unites them but the crime they are about to commit. And she is ignorant of the fact that even the reasons for their being accomplices are as different as the trajectories of their lives.

Dupont

Virgilio Dupont was born in Xinavane of immigrant Mauritian parents who had come there when they were young. He was the youngest of five brothers, which to some extent explained his weak character as he grew up under the obsessive protection of his mother and the disenchanted indifference of his father, who had wanted a daughter. His lack of application caused him to give up studying before completing his business course, and he had become only a mediocre professional.

He met Mena in Angoche, shortly after being transferred there as a Post Office functionary. He desired her as soon he as saw her and, in an insidious manner, began to follow her from a distance, coming to know where she lived, which houses she frequented, and where she did her shopping . . . He also came to know that she was free of amorous attachments, which he found strange, given her disturbing beauty. What he did not know was that besides her radiant face and beautiful body, the refinement and natural astuteness of Mena did not encourage boys of her social class. They were afraid of developing an intimate relationship with a woman who, despite her limited education, always caused them to feel an uneasy sense of inferiority.

Dupont too felt daunted by the girl's serene behaviour and natural sense of style. But the fact that he was Mauritian and, therefore, according to his beliefs, of a superior race, gave him the courage to approach her. She fixed him with her tranquil eyes and answered that he should talk to her parents, which was not at all what he had intended. He wanted only to have a casual but physically satisfying relationship, until his time in Angoche was over.

Taken aback by her response, the man was still able to stammer a few evasive words about the advantages of 'not involving her parents, for now', but immediately realised he would never possess her if he did not concede to her expectations. Thus, though irritated by the request and by his own weakness in acceding to it, he decided to go and speak to Mena's parents, as if his intentions were honourable.

They received Dupont with cool detachment. They gave him permission to date their daughter as if they were granting him an invaluable favour. During the entire process, he felt ridiculed above all by Mena's mother from whom, without a doubt, Mena had inherited her self-possession and sagacity. According to the customs of the land, the father, normally a pleasant person, treated the potential suitor with appropriate haughtiness.

After he had been submitted to a thorough interrogation about his family and professional life, Dupont said goodbye to Mena and her parents with great relief, silently calling them shit-mulatto people, and promising himself that he would never set eyes on them again. Nevertheless, he did not count on the strong sexual attraction that drew him to Mena. He desired her, he wanted her. Soon after leaving work in the late afternoon, the day after meeting her parents, he literally ran to the house of the young girl while cursing himself for his lack of pride.

Thus began a strange relationship which, on various occasions, almost collapsed, because it was based almost entirely on the physical passion that Dupont felt for Mena. She, for her part, accepted the Mauritian, a man much older than herself, because she felt it was her parents' wish. Like the majority of girls in Angoche, she had been brought up to believe she should accept any man her parents deemed worthy as a husband.

And, despite their show of haughtiness, Mena's parents approved of Dupont because he had a permanent job and belonged to a good family. Besides, people from the South had long been regarded as more civilised, and this stood him in good stead. They didn't particularly like him, but they thought he was a good match. Mena could not contradict her parents, but she was far from feeling any particular interest in Dupont, even if his physical appearance – his slender body and thick, shining hair – pleased her. But from the beginning, his behaviour did nothing to inspire feelings of affection. He refused to have a serious conversation with her and never made any reference to their common future. Whenever they went out, he only wanted to drag her into some hidden corner where he kissed and fondled her so roughly that he sometimes left bruises on her body.

Such physical passion, so devoid of affection or understanding, provoked an anguish in the young girl that went very deep because she could not share it with anyone. Not even with her parents, who were still content with the idea of a Mauritian son-in-law, even if he was not proceeding with the wedding arrangements as quickly as they would have liked. One day, when Dupont was rushing her to one of his favourite dark corners, Mena stopped suddenly and said:

'You are not going to marry me. You just want me to be your mistress until you return home, that's all.'

It was neither a complaint nor an implied question but a statement made so firmly that Dupont did not dare reply because he had a strange feeling that Mena could read his mind.

When, finally, he found the courage to face her, he could not but admire her. She seemed very calm as she stared at him with haughty eyes, the colour of night. Just the slight tremor of her bottom lip, full like a ripe fruit, betrayed some apprehension. And her entire being was an oasis of freshness on that scalding January afternoon. Her light dress accentuated her small waist and left exposed the olive-skinned temptation of her cleavage and arms.

'What do you mean?' Dupont stammered, staring at the girl, dizzy with desire.

'That I will never be your mistress. I thought I should warn you, so that you don't waste any more time,' said Mena.

The wedding took place a few months after this short decisive exchange. For the first time in his life Dupont dared openly to oppose his parents, and his family, who could not accept that he had chosen as a wife a mulatto woman from Angoche when there were, in Lourenço Marques, so many daughters of Mauritian families.

During the entire period preceding the wedding, Dupont's mother, familiar with his weak character, bombarded him with letters – at first lamenting, then threatening – and begging him, in a mixture of patois and Portuguese, to give up 'such madness'. He ended up not reading them, obsessed as he was with Mena and determined to marry her. Nonetheless, he hated the idea of marrying beneath him and hated himself for giving way to what he felt to be weakness. Only Mena's great sense of obedience to her parents enabled her to withstand her fiancé's contradictory moods, which could suddenly change from passionate outbursts to aggrieved silence.

Such was their sad engagement, as sad as the very day of their marriage, despite the party that Mena's parents made a point of organising. Dupont, during the entire ceremony, maintained an expressionless, almost distant look, and not even the noisy happiness of the guests and the alcohol he was drinking were able to cheer him up. He felt constrained by a vague sense of not being himself, a sensation perhaps caused by the absence of his family on such an occasion – at which, had circumstances been different, they would definitely have been present. Their absence, despite his confused excuses, also embarrassed Mena's proud mother who occasionally glanced at him, her eyes full of reproach and reprimand.

Dupont and Mena lived on for two more years in Angoche until his contract ended, and then they moved to Lourenço Marques. Dupont's family could not but be impressed by Mena's beauty and innate refinement, but they never accepted her as one of them. She was mulatto and, according to their convictions, of an inferior race.

Mena could not understand the basis of such racist beliefs, considering that all Mauritians looked to her like mulattos, even if some of them had almost straight hair. What, however, she was quick to recognise was that because she was not from Mauritius, she was regarded as no more than an intruder. And she also realised sadly that she could not count on her husband's support, despite his unsatiated lust for her – a passion which, all the same, never overcame his deep subconscious feelings of insecurity in relation to his family.

Virgilio Dupont was, of all the brothers and sisters, the least successful. With his incomplete business course and uncertain character, he was never able to achieve the sang-froid of his brothers, who always treated him with condescension, even contempt. They had completed their studies, even if these were at a basic level, and outside working hours they moonlighted, which allowed them to maintain an acceptable standard of living. Meanwhile, his sisters, who were not blessed with their brothers' good looks, having inherited their father's prominent chin, nevertheless managed to marry 'men of standing' who were, most importantly, Mauritians. Only he, Virgilio, besides being nothing but an obscure, poorly paid civil servant, had brought on his family the 'shame' of having married a mulatto.

So, even without being aware of it, Dupont treated his wife with silent resentment that exploded in fury at the slightest mishap. When he discovered that physically abusing her relieved

51

him, albeit momentarily, of the permanent tension under which he lived, he began to beat her with a violence comparable only to that with which his father used to beat his mother before he became an ailing, but calm, old man.

Mena had somehow learnt to resign herself to these beatings because she knew that a husband's abuse formed part of the destiny of many women. Something, though, had happened to her body, which shut her off from Dupont's caresses and prevented her from having children. She was also losing the aura of pride and self-possession that had always surrounded her. This made her seem more available. Men no longer admired her from a distance but, at the few social gatherings she attended, buzzed around her like bees dizzy with the nectar of an exquisite flower. And Dupont's relatives never lost an opportunity to say that only a woman with such vulgar blood in her veins would prove such an attraction to men.

However, it was due to Mena that Mozambique's independence definitively separated Dupont from his family. His sick father had died, and his mother, brothers, sisters and closest relatives all decided to flee to Portugal. Some provided justification; others simply joined the bandwagon, not wanting to be left behind in a country that everyone else was leaving.

When Dupont told his wife that they too were going to Portugal, she emphatically refused to accompany him. Neither his insults nor his beatings would make her change her mind. So he was unhappily divided between his wish to accompany his family and his desire to hold on to Mena. The latter prevailed, helped by the fact that his siblings did not insist he go with them, afraid that he would prove a burden.

'They think like me!' Mena used to tell him, with uncharacteristic crudeness. 'If you can barely earn enough to eat here, in a strange land you will simply starve. And your family are not likely to support you, and even less me.'

Dupont stayed. He resentfully watched his family make preparations for their journey, tormented by the feeling that if only he had the capacity to make a lot of money, nothing would prevent him from going and taking Mena with him.

At the hour of departure, only his mother seemed to feel any sorrow at leaving him, hugging him in silence and wetting his face with her tears. His siblings, on the other hand, only seemed concerned about missing the plane, hugged him distractedly and promised to send news. After a very long silence, their letters began to arrive. At first they were brief and saturated with a hidden longing; more recently, they had spoken of their achievements, which enabled them to live with a certain abundance. Obviously they never referred to the source of such income – shady deals and sacrifices, which would have been unthinkable in Mozambique.

Far from making him happy, his family's success in Portugal exacerbated the resentment that Dupont felt because he was not 'making the most of life' like his siblings. His suspicion that Mena despised him for the same reason, inflamed his rancour. And so, almost without realising it, money gradually became his new obsession, dominating his thoughts to such an extent that one day a colleague said half-jokingly:

'Listen here, Dupont, you'd kill your own mother for a few bucks, wouldn't you?'

'Not quite. But money is short,' Dupont replied, as if he too were joking.

He did not link this brief dialogue to the tall, dark, thick-set stranger who one day approached him as he was leaving the Post Office, introducing himself as Romualdo Cunha and inviting him to a private chat in a nearby bar. Overcoming a certain reluctance, due to the easy-going, self-confident nature of the unknown man and his own feelings of inferiority, Dupont agreed to accompany him, thus inadvertently changing the trajectory of his life.

'There is no longer a decent place to have a drink in this country,' commented the big man, looking round the room with obvious distaste as they sat down at one of the bar tables.

Dupont made a vague gesture of agreement, waiting in expectant silence for what else the stranger had to say.

'I know you're surprised that I want to speak to you privately. But I think we'll understand each other soon enough,' began Romu, having ordered their drinks.

'We'll see,' Dupont responded cautiously.

'Look . . . we cannot talk openly here and at my house there are too many people. But if we could go to your house I . . .'

'My house?' interjected the Mauritian, suspiciously. 'Why . . .'

'Right now I can only say that I have a good proposition for you. It will mean one thousand five hundred rand a month, as well as bonuses for each job that . . .' Romu continued, quietly.

'But . . . you don't even know me. I don't understand.'

'You're the one that doesn't know me. But I know you. I know who you are and you seem to be the right person for me. Why else would I make you an offer?'

'I still don't understand. Why me?' insisted Dupont.

'From what I know, I think you deserve it. And . . . come on, tell me friend, do you or don't you need the bucks?'

'Every guy needs the bucks . . .'

'Isn't it? Even the rich. And this is real money, not that worthless metical stuff,' responded Romu, looking round cautiously.

Dupont was silent and slowly sipped his beer.

'So . . .' said the other, at last, 'are we going to your house or not, where we can really talk?'

'Let's go,' answered Dupont quickly.

'You do well to grab the opportunity,' concluded Romu in an almost solemn way, glimpsing a flicker of pure greed in the Mauritian's eyes.

When, a short time later, Mena opened the door to the two men, Dupont felt a sudden intense anger at the expression on Romu's face, which was that of a leering wolf. Mena was promptly chased inside the house and the visitor invited to sit down and be brief.

And Romu was brief and to the point. He was not a man who liked to waste time. He stated that he was a South African agent and that South Africa was a fantastic country, a country advanced in everything, governed by people who know what they are doing; a country that just wants to help the Mozambicans to advance from their backwardness. 'Yes,' Romu repeated, he was proud to be an agent 'for such a fantastic country, which, luckily, is so close to Mozambique'. His mission was to recruit more Mozambican agents. And Romu having, coincidentally – 'just coincidentally' – observed Dupont on several occasions, had been given the impression that he could be a good agent. This was because he appeared to be a refined, open-minded person, well ... And so he was offering him one thousand five hundred rand a month, one thousand five hundred, real money ... besides bonuses for each little job he had to do. Being questioned about the nature of 'such little jobs', Romu informed Dupont that there would be nothing much ... just helping with the 'liquidation of certain individuals' who had proved inconvenient to their South African neighbours and friends, who just wanted to help Mozambique ...

The truth was, of course, that Romu had been told about Dupont through one of his colleagues, the same one who, months earlier, had joked that the Mauritian would kill his mother for a few bucks. That man was already an informer and, when he knew that Romu needed more Mozambican agents, indicated that Dupont might be a likely candidate because he was someone who was likely to do anything for money.

'That guy doesn't have a problem. For a buck he'll do anything,' he had said.

'So,' asked Romu, 'are you going try your luck, or not? Real bucks, for doing almost nothing.'

'You know . . . I have never been involved in politics. And also . . . I have never liquidated anyone. Does it have anything to do with those Renamo guys?' said Dupont, indecisively.

'Hey man, do you think I would mix with that mob? I work directly with the South Africans. Renamo are just cannon fodder. The action there is kill or be killed. Us, no, we work clean and safe. You will just have to help when we need you. And when it comes to liquidation, you don't have to do that job . . . your job is to help. Simply help! But . . . I can see that you really don't need the bucks!' replied Romu, feigning impatience and starting to get up, while watching Dupont's reaction out of the corner of his eye. Had he said too much? No. And anyway if Dupont gave him any trouble, he knew how to keep him quiet.

'OK, I accept,' the Mauritian agreed with a finality that masked his anxiety.

'I knew it. You're a refined, cultured guy. I knew you'd accept. We'll meet in a week's time to make the arrangements. I will contact you before then. I don't need to tell you to keep your mouth shut. If not, I don't know what might happen to you. This is serious work . . .'

'Of course . . . of course,' the other hastened to agree.

'Ah . . . I almost forgot. Here's an advance of five hundred rand. That's the way we work, cash up front,' concluded Romu.

With the rand notes sweating in his hands Dupont accompanied Romu to the door, feeling at the same time a strange elation, a mixture of fear and triumph.

◆

But now Mena, sitting alone on the kitchen bench, still doesn't realise that what led Dupont to become an accomplice of the other two was greed for money.

Zalíua

Zalíua was still in Theasse's belly when his father went to the mines of Jone, tired of working from sunrise to sunset without anything to show for it.

'Goodbye, wife, I will send money and news as soon as I can,' he said in farewell.

And then he departed, leaving Theasse leaning against the trunk of a cashew tree her husband had planted next to the hut, and watching as if in a dream as he disappeared like smoke in the mist of dawn. But the promised money never arrived and the news that once in a while spread through the village was contradictory but always alarming. Some informants were emphatic that Theasse's husband had been killed in a rockfall in the mine where he worked, others that he had been murdered during a fight, others still that he had moved in with a fat, ugly South African woman, who was a big party lover, and with whom he would happily get drunk on his days off.

Theasse listened to all these stories more and more absent-mindedly as they were repeated. But as time passed, she was obliged to harvest alone, from her exhausted *machamba*, sufficient food for the three children whom her husband had left behind. In the depths of her heart, a silent bitterness slowly accumulated against the man who had abandoned her and to whom, besides the strength of her arms, she had given pleasure and children. Truly, she never believed that her husband had been killed, but that she had been swapped for the fat, ugly, party lover.

Knowing of her uncertain situation, men circled her hut, desiring her body, which was still fresh and youthful, despite successive pregnancies. Nevertheless, as poor as she was, Theasse did not have the slightest desire to get involved with any such peasant farmers, from whom she could expect nothing, not even financial support. She firmly rejected them, invoking her status as a married woman, one still waiting for her husband, even if deep inside herself she knew that he would never return.

Zalíua was born shortly after his father had left. The only male in a family of women, he grew up treated with deference by his mother and his sisters. From a very early age, he knew how to take advantage of this privileged situation, demanding special attention and reacting violently to any denial. So he developed into a despotic, lazy adolescent who despised work in the fields, considering it labour for women and weak men. His secret hero was his father whom he had never known and who, in his understanding, did well to run away from such misery, even if it meant sacrificing his wife and children.

Theasse observed her son with concern, as he seemed consumed with antipathy for everything around him. Little by little, she realised with fear that one day he too would leave, never to return. Counselled by another village woman renowned for her prudence and wisdom, Theasse sought help from the region's most famous *curandeiro*. After lengthy ceremonies, which drained Theasse of almost all her produce, the *curandeiro* declared that the spirit of a woman had possessed little Zalíua, and was calling on him to join her.

Theasse immediately concluded that the *curandeiro* was referring to the fat, ugly South African woman who loved parties.

His prophecy gave foundation to her conviction that her husband was still very much alive, and living with that fat, ugly female – but one who was no doubt powerful and would erase the memory of his family from her husband's heart. Not content with this, she had now, Theasse believed, succeeded in planting the seed of restlessness in the spirit of her own son. Nonetheless, after the *curandeiro*'s ceremonies, she anxiously hoped that his restlessness would disappear. Zalíua, however, remained the same lazy, troublesome teenager, tormenting her and his sisters with his angry outbursts.

Almost beside herself with worry, Theasse once again sought help from the wise village woman, explaining that although she had wasted almost everything she had on the famous *curandeiro*'s ceremonies, Zalíua's behaviour had not changed and his eyes announced his imminent departure. The prudent old woman listened patiently, and then said simply, 'Give up, Theasse. Give up fighting against that woman. She has already taken your husband and now she wants to take your son as well. It is better to prepare yourself, because one day he will simply leave. That woman has a lot of power.'

'But why does she want my only male child?' cried Theasse.

'Maybe just because he is your only male child,' was the woman's enigmatic answer.

From that moment, Theasse began to have trouble sleeping. Utterly miserable, she did not know whether she preferred wakefulness to a restless sleep poisoned by nightmares in which she appeared leaning against the trunk of the big cashew tree, watching Zalíua slowly disappearing in the morning mist, without once waving, or looking back.

Nights of insomnia and the constant expectation of seeing her nightmares realised left the poor woman physically and emotionally exhausted. She acquired the habit of resting, without moving, for long hours during the day. She allowed herself to become imbued with the still, quiet pain that accompanies the end of hope.

But one day a glimmer of hope returned. Sitting at the door of her hut, Theasse felt her heart lift when she saw Father Cirilo. He was a Catholic missionary, an Italian, who used to visit the villages, trying to recruit followers to his faith. The mission in which he lived was a long way from Theasse's home, but every two months he would appear on his motorbike, to the excitement of the village children who would follow him laughing and chattering. He would stop at every hut and talk with the peasants, sometimes relieving them from their hunger with small donations. He had made a great effort to learn the language of the region and had been generously compensated for his efforts by the warm acceptance of the villagers. Although he did not manage to convert many adults, he succeeded in taking with him their wisest and strongest children who, in exchange for hard work in the mission *machambas*, were converted to the Catholic faith and received a rudimentary but solid education.

On that day Father Cirilo greeted Theasse as he always did, smiling not so much with his mouth but with his childishly clear eyes. And on seeing him like this, so available and so friendly, the idea of giving her son to the church flashed through her head. Not that she had ever wished for Zalíua to go to the mission. But, suddenly, it seemed to her the only way to remove him from the influence of that powerful South African female who, from so far away, still fought for him. 'I would rather give him to the priests than to that woman,' thought Theasse while, in a clear voice, she asked, 'Father, don't you want to take my son Zalíua with you to study at the mission?'

The Father looked at her, perplexed. He was taken by surprise because it was always with great reluctance that the villagers, even those who were starving, allowed their children to accompany him. What upset them was not so much the separation, but the conversion of their offspring to a foreign faith, one that despises ancestor worship and concentrates on a God too complicated for their own liking. Their permission was, in general, the culmination of a long process of persuasion in which the missionary presented them with the perspective of a more hopeful future for their children as Catholics. So, Father Cirilo did not know how to respond to Theasse. Besides, he seemed to recall that Zalíua was a teenager who was known for his aggressive attitude and sullen demeanour.

'Why do you want to send your son to the mission?' he asked, to gain time.

Theasse felt that she should not reveal her true motives. Instead, she pleaded that she was worried about Zalíua's future, condemned, as he was, to grow up without a father's support because, as the priest well knew, she did not want any other man. It was not in vain that Theasse hid what really worried her, while unfurling like a flag her situation as a virtuous, abandoned woman. Her plea, put in this way, moved the kindly Catholic priest. So it was that two months later, Zalíua left for the mission.

During the six years that he lived there, he made progress because he was ambitious and worked hard. He did not take any pleasure in studying but armed himself with knowledge which he assumed he could, much later, turn to his own advantage. Other boys from the school who had done well had gone to Lourenço Marques. In this way he cultivated the approval of the priests whom he tried to please in everything, even the work in the fields, which he hated. He did not want to work on the land.

It was only Father Cirilo who, at times, had the disturbing sensation of glimpsing a hard ambition in the boy's eyes. Nevertheless, nothing concrete ever justified such an intuition. It was, thus, with real sincerity, that Father Cirilo praised the boy in front of his mother on the day he took him home, aged twenty, and having completed a primary school education.

'He was always very well behaved,' he said, 'and as a result we have already found him a job in Lourenço Marques. One month from now he will begin work and will earn money to help you, Theasse. You should be very happy, and grateful to God,' smiled the priest for, despite his occasional misgivings, he was feeling a little smug.

Theasse, though, was a mother: thus what had escaped the priests for years, she intuited in an instant and so she was neither happy nor able to give thanks to God, even though during Zalíua's long absence, she could sometimes barely restrain her desire to see her only son.

The priests would only allow the mission students contact with their family in cases of the deaths of close relatives. They thought that family proximity would negatively influence the boys' education and make it more difficult for them to become good Catholics. So, not even when the boy's two sisters had married, had he come home. During all those long years, Theasse had often imagined the day her son would return, a man freed from the spirit of her fat tormentor in Jone, who would be ready to support her in her old age. But, when she observed Zalíua slinking towards her like a leopard, smiling and showing his wonderful teeth, while extending his hand as if she were a stranger, she saw his eyes were implacably hard, and Theasse knew that she had lost him.

The short time they spent together before he left for the city was painful for both of them. Theasse watched Zalína in a guarded but obsessive way, trying, perhaps, to understand why she still saw in the young man's gestures and looks his desire to abandon her. She asked herself, almost involuntarily, if it had been worth sending him to the mission because it seemed so clear that he was still under the spell of that other woman in

Jone. Zalíua, on the other hand, felt the weight of his mother's probing eyes and avoided her as much as he could, and so the almost tangible chasm that separated them grew wider. It was with great relief that he said farewell and left to begin his new life in Lourenço Marques.

'Goodbye, mother. I will send you money and news, when I can,' were his last words.

Theasse felt a shiver of fear. The words were those of her husband as he departed at dawn so long ago. And, as then, she stood quietly, leaning against the big cashew tree, watching her son who, as in her nightmares, seemed to evaporate into smoke in the mist, leaving without once looking back.

Zalíua caught the train at the station nearest the village and, carefully following all the instructions from the mission's priests, arrived in Lourenço Marques. There he met another priest who took him to his place of employment and arranged what he thought was suitable accommodation for Zalíua.

The boy was delighted by the fact that everything was so easy, as he had somehow expected insurmountable obstacles. He was also thrilled by the city which, to his peasant eyes, shone irresistibly on the edge of the sea, whose immensity and beauty he relished too. He was also delighted with his ability to do, without difficulty, his modest job at the Department of Public Works because, even if he was no more than a lowly messenger, he was proud of his status as an employee.

So he lived in a state of perpetual fascination, his senses receptive to everything around him. And, in the late afternoon, after work, he wandered along the downtown streets, looking into shop windows and gazing, enthralled, at cars and people. He would return, later, tired but happy, to his hut in the township, swallow something to eat and fall into a deep sleep.

But it was not long before such walks turned into a torment for Zalíua because they revealed to him the degree of his indigence and poverty, which would not allow him to possess any of the many things he admired. Soon he also began to tire of being constantly obliged to pay the price of his position as a lowly employee. 'Zalíua fetch this, Zalíua take that, Zalíua, Zalíua, Zalíua.' He was particularly resentful of a Miss Odete, a mulatto woman, who was thin and scrawny, despite a life of eating sandwiches, roasted peanuts and other delicacies that she ordered him to go and buy at the most unpredictable times, as if delighting in the power she had over him.

Increasingly, Zalíua felt the gnawing, frustrating sensation of having gained little by moving to Lourenço Marques because the attractions that the city offered would never be more than temptations. In effect, his wages melted away on small portions of food and on renting the corner in which he slept, in a hut shared with unknown people whose situation was as lacklustre as his own. It was certainly not for this, Zalíua thought, in indignation, that he had spent six long years in the mission, and tired himself out with the books he had found so boring.

So his feelings of fascination and delight were slowly replaced by a barely contained anger, which was reflected in his swaggering walk, his burning eyes and, above all, his smile. A feline smile, in which his very strong beautiful teeth gave the impression of being about to bite. 'There's something about this boy that scares me,' thought Miss Odete, observing his indolent smile and cruel mouth.

Sometimes, in frustration, Zalíua made plans to emigrate to Jone, as his father had done before him. The only thing that stopped him was his fear of the mines to which, he was sure, he would never adapt. Finding no other immediate solution to the prospect of a life of poverty and servitude, he resentfully made the decision to go to night school, which seemed like an admission of failure.

Studying, in itself, he despised. He felt it was a waste of time to learn, for example, that 'chair' is a common noun and that a 'frog' belongs to a class of Amphibia. It seemed to him that very little that derived from books was useful for everyday life. Nevertheless, he enrolled in the fifth class of night school. If he were to succeed, he felt at least he might gain status. Thus he awaited his hour.

In reality, his hour arrived one year after independence, after he had completed the eighth grade, and when he heard, by chance, that the police were recruiting young men into their ranks. He applied and was accepted. Without being subjected to any psychiatric testing, and after a brief training period, he was invested with more authority than he had ever dreamt possible. Being an only son and ambitious, he easily convinced himself that he deserved this authority. The inebriating wine of power went straight to his head, filling it to overflowing with revolutionary slogans which he soon learnt to use for his own benefit.

This being the case he fulfilled his work zealously, but not for the sake of that abstraction called 'the people', for whom he felt nothing but contempt. What gave him pleasure in his new job was the hunt, the camouflaged pursuit, and finally the capture of a so-called 'criminal'. Here, the confirmation of his power over the captured gave him an almost sexual pleasure. In such a manner Zalíua distinguished himself, capturing the guilty and unwary, so that, with less than two years of service behind him, he was given the mission of establishing and heading an office of the Criminal Investigation Police in Nacala. He was only twenty-six years old.

When he arrived at his new posting he soon realised that, in the hierarchy of the local power structure, he occupied a privileged position. Among the important people of the town, only the administrator could oppose him. But this bureaucrat was in fact only the acting administrator and – besides having many weaknesses, most notably to do with women – was only interested in keeping his position for as long as possible. It never crossed his mind to interfere in police activities.

For Zalíua it was a great pleasure to order beautiful *marusse* girls to be sent to prison so that he could rape them in the filthy prison cells; it was a delight to have rich Indians buy their freedom with very expensive hi-fis and large amounts of money – paid in cash; it was a great pleasure to have desirable women pay for the release of their men with their own bodies; and to have marijuana dealers introduce him to their networks and share their profits. He was also deeply gratified to own a house with expensive jambire wood furniture, cars to drive at suicidal speeds, and booze running like water at weekend orgies, and women, many women; and, finally, even a wife, the port captain's delicate, beautiful daughter who had accepted him out of fear.

The complete impunity with which he used and abused his position prevented him from recognising that his downfall would lie in the frail young man with blinking, short-sighted eyes, who confronted him one day.

Zalíua had returned to his studies and the end-of-year exams were approaching. The principal of the town's only secondary school was tired of Zalíua's vengeful persecution of those teachers who were refusing to guarantee that they would give him high marks. The principal decided to make his disapproval clear once and for all.

'I do not want in any way whatsoever to interfere with your studies or your life,' he said on the day he bravely decided to confront Zalíua. 'On the contrary, I wish you success. But I cannot accept your harassment of the teachers at my school, because they give you the marks you deserve. Besides, you rarely attend classes. '

Zalíua could not believe what he was hearing. How could this shit principal dare to defend those teachers who did not want

him, Zalíua, commandant of the PIC, to pass his exams? NO
. . . this old goat could not be right in the head.

'But . . . you, don't you know who you are speaking to? I am
the most senior man in this in town. I am at the top of the pile!
Do you hear?' he said at last . . . in a harsh voice, loud with
indignation.

'I know very well that you are at the top of the pile,' replied
the principal of the secondary school, unperturbed. 'But this
does not give you the right to prevent the teachers from fulfilling
their obligations. They can only give the marks that students
deserve. No bad feelings towards you, but . . .'

'You are under arrest" interrupted Zalíua, getting up suddenly. 'You are under arrest . . . arrested for lack of respect to
the authorities.'

'Do as you wish,' said the other in turn, seeming quite calm.

Dismayed by not sensing the usual smell of fear about the
small man sitting in front of him, Zalíua began to harangue him
about his obligations, his great duty to respect the authorities
and never, but *never*, to play with power.

'Never play with power, do you hear? You want to play with
power but with power you cannot play, do you hear me?' he
repeated contemptuously.

The other man did not seem to hear him, limiting himself to
staring at a distant point in the room.

'You have a very confused mind. And you are going to stay
with us to clear up this confusion,' concluded Zalíua, confused
himself by the unexpected serenity of his visitor.

The principal of the secondary school spent nineteen days in
a tiny empty cell. The nights, without sleep, were shared with
rats, cockroaches, bedbugs and clouds of mosquitoes, which
entered freely through the window. Dawn would find him, his
eyes wide-open, hunched in his corner, still staring at the last
rats running into their holes. During the day, what afflicted him

most was the odour that the whole jail exhaled, much as an animal exhales its own smell. Paradoxically it was a subtle, penetrating aroma, which clung to people and things, and prevented him from eating.

Meanwhile the news of the detention of the principal of the secondary school went off like a bomb in town because nobody believed that he could have committed any crime against the security of the state, as Zalíua would have it. Teachers, students, parents of students, and friends, all tried to offer him their support; but because Zalíua had prohibited all visits, they gathered, as a multitude, in front of the jail. Only his wife had permission to visit him, and then only once a day, to bring him food – because the jail provided no food for the prisoners.

On the seventeenth day of his imprisonment she appeared as usual at the visiting hour. She spread out the embroidered napkin on the ground, set out the lunch tins, and went to sit next to her husband. He felt her sense of latent urgency, but only after he took her wrist with his shaking hand, did she confide:

'Dr Luís Filipe called last night. Everything is going well. The Ministry want a complete report. You should be out in a few days.'

The principal of the secondary school simply closed his blinking eyes, and held his wife's wrist with slightly more strength.

Two days later the telex ordering the immediate release of the principal of the secondary school provoked great agitation in the Provincial Directorate of the PIC in Nampula. Having been hastily summoned from Nacala, Zalíua, dumbfounded, read the order for the man's release, feeling his world shaking around him. How was it possible, he asked himself, astonished, how was it possible that concern about an insignificant school principal could have resulted in the document he had just read, and which ordered him, Zalíua, to release the man immediately?

'And look here, this is an order that must be fulfilled right now – otherwise we are in shit,' warned the PIC's provincial director, a man who, until then, had never dared to challenge Zalíua, because it was said that he was protected by the governor, who shared the same birthplace.

After his release, the principal's main concern was to write the report requested by the Ministry of Education. When it was complete, he went to Maputo to deliver it in person.

The report led to a thorough investigation of Zalíua's life and conduct. And then they spoke: the beautiful *marusse* girls and the rich Indians and the husbands of the desirable women and the teachers and even the marijuana dealers all spoke out. Zalíua was expelled from the police and sentenced to four years in prison. He lived those years grinding his teeth against 'a government of ungratefuls who don't appreciate those who work'.

When released, he decided to return to Maputo. He was a man enraged by destiny. The authorities had confiscated almost everything he had extorted and accumulated over the years. His wife, alleging abuse, asked for a divorce and this was granted. All of his Saturday orgy friends had also disappeared. Only a burning desire for revenge seemed to keep him alive. Day after day, he postponed the mundane task of looking for a job and became an assiduous frequenter of drinking dens where he spent what he had been able to hide from justice and from his ex-wife.

The South African agent who recruited him, also an assiduous frequenter of drinking dens, was soon interested in the lonely, embittered, chain-smoking drinker. Discreetly making enquiries here and there, he discovered his story. There was nothing that suited him better than a discontented former policeman. His approach was prudent but unnecessarily so; Zalíua accepted his proposal without much discussion.

'Sure money every month. And also a bonus for each operation, all in rands,' said the agent from South Africa.

Zalíua toasted him with his cruel white smile and his cold eyes.

'It's not the money that concerns me most. What really grabs me is being able to get my revenge on this shit government. When is the first operation?' he said, thus sealing the pact.

◆

But now Mena, sitting alone on the kitchen bench, will never know that what made Zalíua an accomplice of the other two was a greedy thirst for revenge.

Romu

While still a child, Romualdo already suspected that the mulatto, Mr Pugas, whom he called father, was not really his father. Not because, among all the siblings, he was the only one whose skin was very black, nor because he was discriminated against in any way. Rather, Mr Pugas, a man detached from the rest of the family, seemed to concentrate all his capacity for affection on Romualdo. He worried about his health, his schooling, and even his happiness. Occasionally he passed his rough, bony hand over the child's face, in a gesture of affection. As far as the other children were concerned, their father limited himself to watching them grow up, as if they were domestic animals to whom it was enough to give only the necessary food. And when, sometimes, the others rebelled against his obvious preference for

Romualdo, their mother, always an easy-going woman, tried to appease them, saying that their father liked all of them, and it was just that Romualdo was the eldest.

'Even you have to have respect for him,' she advised.

The others, though, were not eager to respect their brother – a bad student, a troublemaker, and above all, different. Secretly they despised him.

Romualdo grew up amid the conciliatory kindness of his mother, the jealous animosity of his brothers and the strange affection of Mr Pugas. Paradoxically, the more he realised that he was the sole object of the man's affection, the more he doubted that he was his father. Finally, his doubts disappeared one particular morning, one that marked a new type of relationship between him and the rest of his family.

He had woken up with a sweet laziness of body and a nausea that seemed to jump from his stomach to his head but, encouraged by his mother, he managed to dress and go to school. He had never hated the classroom so much or the teacher who walked in a leisurely way from one side of the classroom to the other, dictating. Romualdo felt an intense desire to tell her to shut up. He concentrated so hard on restraining this desire that he did not notice the nausea rising from his stomach to his throat. Suddenly he vomited all over his exercise book. Then he began to shake, as the sickness was replaced by an unbearable cold.

When, shortly afterwards, Romualdo, authorised by the teacher, arrived home, the house seemed immersed in silence. His brothers were at school, but he found it strange that his mother was not working about the house, and went to look for her in the bedroom. The room was locked from the inside but, despite his knocking and calling, nobody answered him.

He decided to go and lie down as his body was demanding a bed. Walking away, though, he had the distinct impression of hearing hushed murmuring, which intrigued him and helped him to forget that he was feeling ill. He went to his room, but had the foresight to leave his door slightly open, in a way that allowed him to see anyone who passed along the corridor coming from his parents' bedroom. A short while later, he saw his mother sneak out on tiptoe, followed by a white man whom he recognised as one Sergeant Cerca. 'Now I know that Mr Pugas is not my father,' was the first thought that arose in his confused brain before he fell into a deep sleep. When he woke, it was already late afternoon. Dona Elsa was sitting near the bed.

'I saw,' Romualdo's eyes said immediately.

'I know that you saw,' the answer lay in his mother's eyes, the softest feature on her stern face.

From that moment Romualdo felt relieved of a great burden because everything about his family became clear. His mother went to bed with any man she chose. She had also slept with his real father, who was probably as black as she was. Mr Pugas, as he had always suspected, was not his father and the four little mulatto kids he called brothers were just his half-brothers.

As a result, he experienced a sensation of painful liberation. A strange freedom, but one that allowed him to challenge the authority of his parents, mainly that of his mother, over whom he came to have limitless power. The first time he became aware of this was just a few days after he had seen his mother sneak out on tiptoe, followed by Sergeant Cerca.

That afternoon, as was his habit, Romualdo went down to the quay and, as sometimes happened, a boat just outside the bay – its lights glowing mysteriously – seemed to be calling to him irresistibly. He was always jealous of people who, amidst noisy excitement, boarded the small boats with outboard engines, which took them to the ships anchored beyond the shallow harbour. He had never been lucky enough to accompany them, but that afternoon, taking advantage of the confusion, he ran down the quay's slippery stairs and jumped into one of the small boats that was about to leave. The boat was already half way across the bay, when the ticket collector asked him for money for the fare. He calmly answered that he had left his money at home. The ticket collector, who knew him by sight, having often seen him wandering along the quay when the boats came in, accepted his excuse and, when they arrived at the ship, let him board. Once there, Romualdo opened every door of the ship except those that were locked from the inside or from which he was chased away. He saw cabins, dining rooms, pantries, kitchens, smoking rooms, bars, and the small disco for the first-class passengers where locals he knew by sight were dancing. Enthralled, he explored the whole ship until he came to a cabin where a few members of the crew seemed to be celebrating around a table loaded with food and bottles of alcohol.

'Come in, little black boy, come, come, celebrate with us!' one man called out as Romualdo opened the door.

'Come in, come in! Oh what a cute little black gatecrasher, come in,' said another. They were all slightly drunk.

It was already supper time and the idea of eating was very attractive to Romualdo. He entered and stood near the table. The men found him a seat and plied him with food and drink, and bombarded him with questions.

At first Romualdo drank the mixture of strong wine and cold water that they gave him with reluctance. But, as he became used to the taste, and the feeling of euphoria it provoked, he began to down each glass with an ease that greatly amused the crew. These men were uneducated Portuguese, given to debauchery. They encouraged the child into speaking and he, emboldened by the wine and the excitement of the adventure, answered them with provocative agility, much applauded by all.

Romualdo never came to know what the Portuguese crew were celebrating, nor who told them where he lived, nor how they took him home. He woke up in his room, late the next morning, with a violent headache that kept him in bed until the next day. When he had recovered from his first hangover, his mother, with an expression of great severity, asked him where he had been until dawn, why he had got so drunk, and who the men were who had brought him home. His response was simply to stare threateningly at her. In this way, his first adventure, like all those that followed, remained unpunished.

Not surprisingly, his brothers found their mother's apparent indifference to their eldest brother's troublesome behaviour very strange. They could only resign themselves to Dona Elsa's increasingly bad moods, and tolerate the reprimands and punishments that she inflicted upon them. Romualdo, on the other hand, hardly noticed that his brothers existed, even though he slept in the same room. If he thought about them at all, he rather despised them because he had secrets to which they had no access unless he wished it.

Meanwhile, he neglected his studies, failing his exams two years running, and finally leaving primary school at the age of fourteen. Mr Pugas would have liked to enrol him in the new Commercial School, but Romualdo's poor results made this impossible. Instead, and as a result of persistent solicitation, he was able to place him as an apprentice in the prosperous firm of M.B. Fortes.

Once there the boy had the good fortune to find, in the manager of the firm, a true master. Making something of Romualdo became for him a major challenge when he realised that, unlike the majority of his other employees, this adolescent, who had barely completed fourth grade, absorbed everything he taught him like a sponge and responded well to being singled out.

That Romualdo was black was not an obstacle to the manager

of the firm. At that time, in order to undermine Frelimo, the colonial government encouraged the promotion of 'good darkies'. The manager's efforts were, therefore, well rewarded by the passion with which Romualdo applied himself to his work, to the astonishment of everybody who knew him.

'Who would've thought,' commented Mr Pugas with barely concealed pride and not a little naivety. 'It seemed he was good for nothing, except parties, but now the boy is showing his mettle. All he needed was a vocation.'

Romualdo was, in fact, genuinely interested to learn in a situation where he was rewarded. So, by the time he was twenty-one, the age at which he was called into military service, he was already assistant to the clerk.

Mr Pugas faced Romualdo's summons into the army with mixed feelings of pride and annoyance. He, like all mulattos of his time, had been prevented from entering the military simply because he was a mulatto. Now, having a son in the army, just like a white man, was a source of great pride, even though he knew that this was only possible because of Frelimo. On the other hand, it did not please him that Romualdo had to interrupt his promising career at M.B. Fortes.

As far as the young man was concerned, he accepted military service as an adventure, particularly when he was selected for the commandos, an élite unit famous for its audacity and extreme cruelty. At the end of his training, however, he no longer saw the army as a simple adventure. His body and spirit had been moulded to fight 'the *terrs*' and their supporters with an unimaginable fury. He could not believe that a 'mob of miserable kaffirs' wanted to be independent instead of being grateful that the Portuguese had assumed the responsibility of governing them. Yes, he was black, but he could see well what was what, and, therefore, he would give anything to be white. He had been trained to be a good commando.

During the years he was in the army, the Island of Mozambique was transformed into a kind of rest camp for commandos deployed in the north of the colony. Periodically they went there to recuperate and, as compensation for their deeds and massacres, they had at their disposal the sea of scandalous blue, sun, peace, fresh food and perfectly beautiful prostitutes. As a result Romualdo had several opportunities to go to his birthplace to rest. He was always received with great demonstrations of affection by his family and by other *assimilados*, to whom he recounted, without a shadow of remorse, stories of the atrocities he had committed. He boasted about burning huts with people alive inside them, disembowelling pregnant women and killing children by throwing them into the air and catching them on the point of his bayonet, and all because people were suspected of supporting Frelimo. He bragged, above all, about his precious collection of '*terrs*' ears', which he himself had cut off and kept as trophies of war. He also told, even if he purposefully omitted some passages, the story of the old woman who could barely walk and who, for months, deceived the whole company of commandos, and whom he, Romualdo, had unmasked. This was the true story:

From the barracks where the company was based they could see the only access road to the nearest village. In the beginning not even Romualdo paid attention to the old woman who used to pass by with a bundle on her head, always accompanied by a child aged about ten. But at a certain stage he grew suspicious of her many comings and goings. He did not share his suspicions with anyone because he did not like exposing himself to ridicule. One day, though, he decided to question the old woman. He walked slowly down the road with the casual air of someone enjoying the morning's fresh air, and the old woman appeared, as always, bundle on her head, child at her side.

She walked with a tired step, in contrast to the proud expression on her face furrowed with wrinkles. She looked straight ahead, not seeming to notice Romualdo's presence. The child, however, seemed apprehensive and instinctively moved closer to her side. Romualdo greeted them and, with false kindness, asked if he could see what was in the bundle. The old woman, instead of answering him, took the bundle from her head and passed it to the child, saying in Quimane:

'Run and take it where you should. Run, grandson!'

It was all so fast and unexpected that Romualdo was left like a statue in front of the old woman who faced him challengingly, while the child disappeared like a ray of light into the thick bush.

'It's munitions that you normally carry in your bundle? Munitions for the *terrs*, isn't it?' interrogated Romualdo, who recovered himself fast.

To all his questions the old woman answered with an obstinate silence and a grimace. Finally, a half-smile blossomed on her withered lips and, after spitting on the ground in a gesture of infinite disgust, she said simply, in her native tongue:

'You nigger son of a bitch.'

Romualdo lost control and all the fury he felt at what the old black woman represented – race, mother, *terr* – were concentrated in the well-aimed blow with his rifle butt which reduced her cranium to an unshapen mass.

'Old bitch! But she also got what she deserved,' he invariably concluded, after he had told his version of the story.

Romualdo's prestige grew among the commandos after the

case of the old woman. He was commended in front of the whole company for his 'high degree of military astuteness and patriotism'. And again when he was honoured and presented by his commander as a symbol of a 'united and indivisible Portugal', and again when his colleagues patted him on the back and affectionately called him Romu, the more he felt certain of the stupidity of the *terrs'* cause.

When he finished his military service, after what had felt like exalted years in the army, besides the nickname Romu, with which he was now familiar, he had an unshakeable conviction of the superiority of the white race and of the absolute necessity of the Portuguese governing Mozambique for always and forever.

By that time he had also heard, mainly from one old friend of Mr Pugas, a man given to sentimental confidences, the truth about his birth. He did not know everything, but at least he knew the gist of what had happened all those years ago . . .

Even when she'd been a teenager Dona Elsa had had the same stern features and the same rough, monotonous drawl that she had as a woman. But these disguised an aura of something profoundly sensual and feminine, qualities that drew men to her like a magnet. They besieged her and lavished her with attention, which she received with an assumed indifference while slowly becoming aware of her power over the opposite sex. It was only later that she realised she was attracted to men with the same intensity as they were to her.

When she was seventeen years old she fell deeply in love with Romu's father. He was a black man with a smooth tongue, godson of Mr Adalberto Madeira, owner of the most exclusive fashion shop on the island and well known for his offbeat tastes in sexual matters. Sharp tongues used to say that even his affection for his black godson was nothing more than a way of repaying favours to the child's father, his cook and his lover.

What is certain is that he sustained and educated his godson, fed him and dressed him perfectly, and even took him for rides in the late afternoon, placing the boy at his feet in his white upholstered rickshaw. He had given him his own name and, later, sent him as a boarder to the trade school on the island, where the boy learnt the work of a printer.

When Elsa fell in love with the young Adalberto, he was still studying. But the money that his white godfather had given him allowed him, once in a while, to leave the boarding school well dressed, with good shoes and a smell of eau-de-cologne, to go and meet his girl. It was an attraction simultaneously violent and sweet, facilitated by Elsa's permissive mother, until the day on which the young woman discovered that she was pregnant.

Just the idea that her father, an *assimilado* and conservative black, would discover that she had become pregnant by a student at the trade school, one still without a profession and the son of a cook to boot, made Elsa feel faint. So, once again, she relied on the astute complicity of her mother, who, knowing her own husband, tried to avoid a tragedy. And it was certainly her astuteness that led her to approach Mr Pugas, a man already in his thirties who used to come to the house frequently to chat with Elsa's father.

To a woman as experienced as Elsa's mother, the covert but intensely desirous looks that Mr Pugas gave her daughter had not gone unnoticed. And it was the certainty that he desired Elsa which one day gave her courage to take advantage of her husband's brief absence, and whisper to Mr Pugas in Macua:

'Elsa is pregnant by a kid who cannot marry her. If her father knows, he will kill her.'

As she predicted, the man offered to assume the role of saviour of Elsa's honour and life. A few days after the unexpected confidence, he formally asked for the young girl's hand in marriage. And the father rejoiced at the prospect of his daughter marrying a mature man with a steady job, and above all, a mulatto.

'My daughter will improve the race,' he told everyone to whom he announced the news.

On the other hand, his wife felt tremendous relief. Elsa too was relieved for she feared her father's retributive anger. For a while, though, the pain of her longing for Adalberto seemed unremitting. But, out of fear, she never went to meet him again. Mr Pugas was all tenderness, and slowly she was able to put her young suitor behind her, though she would never forget him or the passion he had felt for her.

◆

The marriage took place as soon as it was possible. A few months later Romualdo was born. Although a strong baby he was presented to everyone as being premature. Nevertheless, Mr Pugas formed a special attachment to his stepson, a boy who everyone suspected was not his son but whom he had adopted as his own, from the day on which Elsa's mother had prudently confided in him. In his detached way, he loved his young wife, forgiving her infidelities, as someone forgives the mischievousness of a daughter. He considered that as an older man he was fortunate to have acquired such a young wife.

Elsa knew how to take advantage of her husband's benevolence, perhaps to compensate herself for the loss of Adalberto, who had abandoned the island. And even as she grew older, her face sterner and her body heavier, she rarely passed up any opportunity when men responded to her magnetic appeal. This is what had happened on the day on which her son had seen her sneaking out of the bedroom followed by Sergeant Cerca. However, on that occasion, she had awoken in her son a deep hatred that insidiously came to embrace the whole black race, and was exacerbated by Romu's years in the army. 'I was born black by mistake,' he often said to himself.

This is also why, even if he felt no love for her, Romu chose for his wife a woman with sunken cheeks and ruined teeth, but one who was almost white. Immediately after the marriage he left with his wife for Lourenço Marques, partly to break away from his mother and his lighter-skinned siblings and partly because he thought a big city would offer him more opportunities to progress. And it was here that 25 April[1] came to meet him.

Difficult times, for him, of amazement and anger at the 'stupid people's euphoria' that vibrated in the air. Had all that he had learnt in the army been in vain – the sleepless nights, the long marches through forests and over mountains, the haunting fear of *terrs*, who attacked and disappeared like ghosts? And the children whom he had thrown in the air and who had smiled at him, scared and thrilled at the same time, before he disembowelled them with the point of his bayonet, and the screams of those burnt alive in the huts that he set alight, and the ears he had collected, all little black ones he had cut off, and the mulatto woman whose skin was so light, whom he married without love, just to make his children whiter; had all this been in vain?

Until the day of Independence, Romu hoped that something would happen to put an end to the nightmare in which he lived. But nothing happened and on the eve of independence, he tried to drown the frustration that was consuming him in alcohol. He drank until he lost consciousness and when he woke up, Mozambique was already an independent country.

[1] 25 April 1974 – date of the Carnation Revolution in Portugal when a military coup overturned the Salazar regime and installed a democratic government which led to the independence of Portugal's five African colonies.

He never accepted it and when, a few years later, he was contacted by a half-Portuguese South African to join a network of South African agents who operated in Mozambique, carrying out missions of sabotage and terrorism, Romu accepted immediately.

◆

But now Mena, sitting alone on the kitchen bench, is unaware that what made Romu an accomplice of the other two was hatred of his own race.

23.00 HOURS

In the home of Narguiss

'Speak a little more softly,' Muntaz begs, turning up the volume on the Xirico radio that is on the top shelf of the kitchen cupboard.

'There she goes again with the news! It's always the same thing. I don't know why she listens to the news all the time,' mumbles Dinazarde, in the pantry.

Rábia and cousin Fauzia grumble too. 'What an obsession . . . listening to the news, which interests nobody. For me, at least, it's not interesting,' remarks Fauzia, in a provocative tone.

It annoys her to have to interrupt a stimulating conversation about the farewell party she plans to hold, just to listen to the news. This only mentions war, hunger or tedious events, that have nothing to do with them and their lives, she thinks.

'At least thirty men, women and children,' says the newsreader, 'were murdered, and an indeterminate number kidnapped, when a group of armed men attacked a bus on National Road Number 2. The attack took place near Manhiça. According to the survivors, the group was well armed and mostly made up of children between twelve and sixteen years old.' The voice of the newsreader continues, devoid of emotion, serene, apparently indifferent to the bloody fate of thirty victims and the indeterminate number of kidnapped.

By the time the international news comes on, Fauzia and her cousins are again talking and laughing loudly, having returned to the conversation about the farewell party. But Muntaz, quite unable to resign herself to the regularity of the killings and massacres, cannot comprehend her sisters' and Fauzia's high spirits.

'When will it all end? Twelve-year-old children killing...' she wonders.

No one listens, not even her mother, who is absorbed in her own grief.

'Cousin Narguiss,' asks Fauzia, a little later, hearing her repeated sighs, 'are you so sad because cousin Abdul hasn't arrived yet?'

Sighing even more deeply, Narguiss confirms that this is the case.

'It's probably the planes. In this country, a timetable means nothing. Or perhaps he couldn't get a seat. These days the planes are always full,' says Fauzia, in an attempt to console her cousin.

She does not believe what she says, however. She knows about Abdul and his plans. She knows that if he really wanted to spend Eid with his family, he would have done so, even if it meant travelling in an aeroplane packed like a sardine can.

'It's nothing of aeroplane,' Narguiss complains. 'It's because of that woman, you knows. And we here, day of Eid, without father, without husband, like some poor orphan.'

'And without lights ... tomorrow will be like every other day,' interjects Muntaz, trying to change the direction of the conversation.

Over the previous two months Maputo has daily been deprived of electricity, from seven in the morning until eight at night, due to the constant sabotage by Renamo of the high voltage lines that supply the city.

'I really don't know how the food in the fridge doesn't rot,' laments Dinazarde.

'Well *I* won't have to put up with it for much longer. In Lisbon there are no power cuts,' boasts Fauzia.

'Better finish this talk, Fauzia,' says Narguiss, afraid that a new argument will arise between Muntaz and her cousin. The older woman worries constantly about her youngest daughter who, in her opinion, is so intelligent when it comes to books, and so hopeless when it comes to life.

'It's very danger, daughter,' she warns whenever she can. 'We never to know, best to stay quiet, to leave others to do as they are wanting to. To be a thief, leave to be a thief, want to go away, let to go away.'

At that moment, however, her anxiety is unfounded because Muntaz is not concerned about her cousin's provocation. What worries her most as she fries the *gilebes* is her mother's unhappiness, expressed so poignantly through her large clumsy body. 'It's not fair to make her suffer like this, now that she is old and fat and ugly,' the girl thinks rebelliously. 'It's like stealing her last hold on life, on happiness.'

Meanwhile, in the pantry next door, the conversation takes a more stimulating turn towards possible future husbands among the men they know, and details of their physical appearance, manner of dress and the cars they own . . .

Narguiss notices, with regret, that Muntaz remains detached from it all. She would give the last days of her life for her youngest daughter to be like the others, a true woman, one who worries about 'grabbing a husband'. Muntaz, though, only seems to turn good fortune away. Good suitors are not in short supply. With the last one there was even an unpleasant misunderstanding.

The boy belonged to a rich, established Indian family from Nampula, who extended their business network by establishing a branch in Maputo. The young man met Muntaz through mutual friends and was immediately attracted to her, perhaps because of the contrast between the softness of her features and her strong personality, and he soon began to pay the family regular visits. But to his great disappointment, he was usually received by Dinazarde, so he would politely stay to talk for a while, partly out of courtesy but always hoping that Muntaz might return home. She, meanwhile, rarely joined her older sister, while the latter entertained the boy with the friendliness due to a man she viewed as a likely future husband for herself.

During the holidays, however, Muntaz had more free time, so the young man visited them with even greater frequency. Influenced by his own feelings, he interpreted Muntaz's more relaxed attitude, and kindly manners, to mean that she had a deeper interest in him. So, one afternoon when he was alone with her, while Dinazarde was still making herself beautiful, he abruptly confessed that he loved her. Astonished, Muntaz told him he ought to be ashamed of himself, because not only had he misled her sister for months, he now wanted to mislead her as well. And she left the room, leaving her ex-future brother-in-law choking on his own words.

And this was how Dinazarde found him, when she came down with her painted face and carefully coiffured hair. Feeling abandoned and afflicted, the young man began, naively, to beg her to explain to her sister that, as Dinazarde well knew, there was nothing between the two of them, and Muntaz was the woman of his dreams . . .

Dinazarde was deeply offended. How could she, she asked him, explain to Muntaz that there was nothing between them? What about the long hours spent getting dressed for him, putting on make-up, doing her hair for him, waiting for him, talking to him? It was no longer possible for her to bear the presence of this man who was now treating her as if she was nothing. Screaming, she went towards him and threw him out on the street, telling him never to darken their door again – an order with which the perplexed and unhappy young man complied.

For a while the relationship between the two sisters was tense.

Muntaz explained over and over again that she had also been taken by surprise by the extraordinary declaration of love from the presumed future brother-in-law, but Dinazarde found a certain comfort in accusing her of deception, blaming her for having purposely seduced *her* suitor. But today, thanks to the patient intervention of Narguiss, the two sisters are able to laugh, remembering the astonished boy's face, on the afternoon on which they had both banished him from their lives.

And there had been others, not really banished but discouraged by the obstinate Muntaz who now, to the great displeasure of her mother, keeps herself aloof from the 'stimulating' conversation between her sisters and her cousin Fauzia.

It is already past midnight when the girls decide to go to bed. They say goodnight sleepily, anxious for the next day because Eid is still awaited by them with an expectation rooted in their childhood. It contains all the ritual of wearing new dresses, and the visits for the exchange of delicacies between family and friends.

'Mother, come and sleep too. Tomorrow we'll wake up early and finish off everything else that needs to be done,' Muntaz suggests kindly.

But Narguiss does not want to go to sleep, even though her body is begging for rest. She doesn't want to. She does not have the courage to confront the large bed, empty of the presence of the always desirable Abdul, on the eve of Eid. She prefers to continue occupying her hands and her head with preparations so as not to think about her husband who, far away, sleeps with another woman. And she is so lost within herself that, immediately after finding herself alone, her memory flees to the past where, subconsciously, she tries to locate herself. She remembers, with unexpected clarity, a childhood spent in a big house in Matibane, where her father traded in copra and cashew nuts that came from his enormous plantations. Her mother was a quiet mulatto woman who shared her affection equally among her seven children, two boys and five girls.

Narguiss, much like her sisters, was brought up as a 'true woman', that is to say, inside the house and the vegetable garden, chattering happily with her sisters, her ayahs and her friends. She never went to school and still speaks a mangled Portuguese, just like her sisters and friends among her own generation. But she did learn to cook exquisitely, with the ultimate objective of pleasing the man who would one day choose her for his wife.

And they were many, the men who wanted her, attracted by her wonderful body and by her father's fortune. He, though, chased them off as if they were bothersome insects, until finally accepting as his son-in-law the first-born of an Indian man like himself, a very rich landowner, Latifo Remane Satar. Narguiss was then sixteen. The wedding celebrations remained vivid in the memories of those who took part in them.

In the open space in front of her father's large house, canvas marquees were erected, decorated with archways of woven palm fronds, garlands of bougainvillaea and red acacia flowers. For three days and three nights, sheltered by the marquees, the more than five hundred guests ate and drank to the sound of music from the most famous groups from the Island and from Nampula, hired for the event. From the enormous kitchen came: the samosas and the *bagias*, the *rotis*, the pulau rice, the coconut and *oloco* bean rice, the *macua*-style fried fish, the *nimino* fish stew with cassava and sweet potato, the prawn and crab curry, the beef and goat curry, the flame-grilled chicken with coconut milk, the fish and duck *tocassado* curry, the roast veal on a kebab, the *molinoli* bean dish, the *sirisiri matapa*, the cassava leaf with cashew nut *matapa*, the shredded lettuce salad, the carrot and onion chutney, the *sanana* cakes, the monkey-banana fried in sugar and cinnamon syrup, the *massuco* pumpkin sweets, the rice and *mapira mucate* cakes, the *torritorri* sesame sweets, the fried *gilebe*, the *mahaza* sweets of semolina, the *quirre* of fried vermicelli . . . And also the juice of sweet cashew fruit, the fresh coconut milk, the cold drinks. And, especially for the Christians and 'degenerate' Muslims, the fermented cashew-nut juice and other alcoholic drinks.

For the battalion of people who were working in the kitchen and were serving the guests, there was no shortage of *caracata chima* with fish *tocossado*, the only delicacy capable of completely filling their unsophisticated stomachs.

Narguiss still remembers every detail of this rich feast, but mainly she recalls the interminable hours she spent waiting for the groom, seated on the platform specially prepared for her, surrounded by her bridesmaids. She was suffocating beneath the red veil, which the groom would lift when, at last, the lengthy ceremonies forbidden to women had ended.

She also remembers the sea of people eating and drinking at the wedding reception. She could hardly distinguish between the mist of tiredness and the dust lifted by the burning north wind, despite the shelter of the canvas tent. Oh yes, and she can still feel the weight of the jewellery offered to her by the groom's family: the tiara that fastened her hair, the dangling earrings, the necklaces, the bracelets that covered her arms from wrist to elbow, the rings, truly ostentatious and made of solid gold set with emeralds, sapphires and diamonds, brought from Zanzibar and even from India. She also still remembers the occasional sidelong glances of the groom, seated next to her – glances whose malicious significance she only came to understand much later. But then, during the reception, they only made her feel rather anxious.

Now, Narguiss' memory refuses to advance. Refuses to relive those first lonely nights again, waiting in vain for her husband, who would finally arrive at dawn, smelling unmistakably of other women. And the pain of seeing her jewellery, which she had triumphantly shown off on her wedding day, disappear piece by piece, pilfered by her husband. And the humiliating pity of her friends who came to tell her on whose arm her bracelets were tinkling and on whose neck her solid gold necklaces were shining. And still the pain of having to hide her despair from her family, partly from shame and partly out of sorrow for causing them so much suffering.

Others, though, took on the role of telling her family of her husband's exploits, above all of his relationship with a black woman called Sarifa, who had been his mistress for years and with whom he had slept the night following his wedding. Such news truly provoked too much pain for Narguiss' old father who, one day, decided to fetch his daughter and take her back home.

Even now, after almost thirty years, she shakes with embarrassment on remembering that final episode of her life with her first husband. Her father asking, almost with humility, for him to let her leave, at once, for certainly it seemed he no longer wanted her. And the haste with which her husband accepted the proposition, as if he had been wishing for this to happen for a very long time. She, sitting in silence, between the two men, watching them deciding on her destiny as if it didn't belong to her.

In the big house in Matibane, Narguiss was received with the humiliating demonstrations of sympathy that are given to rejected women. For two years she lived voluntarily in confinement, only going out to assist at the funeral ceremonies of close relatives.

It was, coincidentally, at the funeral of a brother-in-law that Abdul, her present husband, saw her for the first time. He later confessed to her that he immediately liked her, not just because of her beauty but also because of her sadness which seemed to surround her in an aura of mystery. So he desired her, not just for her body, but also to console her in her unhappiness. This feeling, completely new to Abdul, who usually wanted nothing from women but confirmation of his own virility, made him live in a state of such excitement that it could only end in marriage. As far as Narguiss was concerned, she accepted the dark-skinned, almost unknown man, only to fulfil her destiny as a woman.

They were joined together in a simple ceremony, nothing like Narguiss' first marriage. The wedding night was also different because Abdul was able to awaken in her the pleasure that had remained unknown to her throughout the two years of marriage to her previous husband. In contrast to her former husband who possessed a kind of impatience, Abdul caressed her with great tenderness combined with such passion that she herself was surprised by the spontaneous response of her body.

When, much later, she found out that, despite such great love, her husband had mistresses, Narguiss convinced herself that it was her destiny to share her man with other women and decided that she would, all the same, be happy with Abdul. He always surrounded her with tenderness and comfort, even in times of crisis, such as now. So she continued to love him with the same astonished gratitude with which she had loved him on that distant night when he taught her to be a woman.

Loving him, despite everything, was also, for her, a way of forgiving herself for her body, now deformed by obesity: a fatness that had grown upon her, slowly and insidiously, after the birth of her second daughter. In vain Narguiss had fought against it, bearing starvation diets, immediately followed by periods of bulimia. But the amorous adventures of her husband drove her to look for compensation in sweet delicacies. These provided her with an immediate if temporary solace for her long years of suffering, but they made her a little fatter with each mouthful.

Today it is no longer possible to recognise, in this large woman, the slender girl that Abdul once knew. Because of this Narguiss forgives him his infidelities and accepts him when he seeks her out, happy and thankful that he still desires her now – without passion, it's true – but with the same disquieting tenderness. Tenderness she is very afraid to lose. And it is this great fear that keeps her in the kitchen, following the thread of her life, far from the big empty bed which makes Abdul's absence on this eve of Eid so terribly difficult to bear.

In the home of Leia and Januário

As always, Leia wakes to the eleven o'clock news. No other alarm would be more reliable than the voice of the newsreader at this time. To begin with the soothing voice barely penetrates her young woman's sleep but gradually it enters her consciousness until it has woken her completely, as if she had slept an entire night. This has been a kind of ritual since they moved into the flat. At around ten o'clock Leia goes to bed with her husband and sometimes, in the middle of a conversation, falls asleep like a baby, until the eleven o'clock news. At first Januário would get upset, mainly when the subject of conversation interested him. 'You don't pay attention to what I am saying,' he would complain and Leia would assure him this was not the case, and that she was really paying attention, but that she fell asleep without meaning to. As time passed, Januário was persuaded that this was true, and he no longer became upset. Instead, he made the most of these moments of silence to read or simply to contemplate the woman peacefully asleep at his side like a child. Occasionally he had to restrain a violent desire to kiss her full lips and her long, beautiful eyelashes. 'When you are asleep, you look like a lovely old-fashioned doll, with your long curled eyelashes,' he has told Leia more than once, and the comparison always makes her feel shy. Januário is not the kind of man who worries much about analysing his own feelings. But when he watches his wife sleeping, it is as if he has gained new insight into his love for her and his increasing desire to make her happy. Despite their difficult life, the endless deprivations, the violence . . . Violence that is now coldly and serenely reported by the voice of the newsreader and which little by little arouses Leia from her slumbers.

She frees herself totally from sleep, just in the middle of the brief description of the massacre perpetrated on National Road Number 2, near Vila de Manhiça. Another massacre like the many that take place daily throughout the country. An occurrence, which, due to its regularity, has already become a banality. But not for Leia, who still feels a sense of horror, not just on behalf of the dead, wounded, kidnapped and displaced, but also for her husband who now listens to the news, his eyes fixed, his jaw clenched and rigid, signs that always indicate tension. Slowly, almost timidly, she reaches for his hand and holds it in hers in silence. 'I'm here, I know what you're suffering,' is what she wants to say with her gesture. 'I know, I know,' he answers, pressing her fingers, silently.

Although he doesn't talk about it, Leia knows that the reports of the massacre still pain her husband as they bring back memories of that long distant night when his parents were burnt alive, screaming, inside their hut, and his village vanished from the face of the earth. She also knows that such reports reinforce his absurd remorse for being left alive. Leia knows all this, not because she is gifted with great intelligence, but due to an intuition born of her love for him, which allows her to know, by a gesture, an expression, Januário's most intimate feelings.

'When is this going to end?' she groans softly to herself, still referring to the massacre, which the newsreader has just finished reporting.

As if she was waiting for these words, little Iris breaks into a wail. She sits up in her little bed next to her parents, crying and rubbing her eyes with her clenched fists.

'I don't know what's the matter with this child today. Even this afternoon she was niggly, but she doesn't have a fever and it doesn't seem as if she is in any pain . . .' comments Leia, rushing to change her daughter's nappy.

'Maybe she's predicting misfortune!' mutters Januário.

'Come on, Januário! More misfortune? We already have everything in this country – war, misery, everything,' protests Leia, trying to calm her daughter.

She walks up and down with the child in her arms and then tries to persuade her to drink some milk that she brings in from the kitchen. The little girl continues to cry, choking on her own sobs and inconsolably rubbing her eyes. It's almost midnight when, at last, she falls into an agitated sleep, whimpering and tossing and turning, shaken by strange convulsions.

'I've lost my sleep!' laments Leia, when, exhausted, she lies down next to her husband. 'I just hope that she hasn't sensed something evil.'

'No. No nothing like that! Can't you see I was just joking?' Januário calms her, nestling her in his arms.

She lets herself lie there, not moving, enjoying this moment of pure tenderness without the slightest implication of sensuality.

'Did you know they have already chosen the winners of the literary contest?' says Januário after some time, breaking the enchantment.

Leia would like to remain with the silence, comforted in her husband's arms, but she knows that the literary contest is important for him and she encourages him to continue. Januário is a night-school teacher and the literary contest is one of the activities at the school which truly gives him pleasure.

It all began shortly after they moved into the flat. To be able to buy the proper food for his daughter, which is only available in the *candonga*, Januário was obliged to find other sources of income besides his job at João Ferreira dos Santos Company. It was in this way that despite lacking the required qualifications, he dared to apply for a job as a teacher of Portuguese. And, due to the dire shortage of such teachers, he was accepted.

To his great surprise, what at the outset appeared just another burden soon became an unexpected source of satisfaction. He discovered that, in teaching, everything pleased him. Preparing the lessons, communicating with students, encouraging them to learn, correcting their tests, marking – everything gave new colour to the grey monotony of his days as a lowly worker in a commercial firm. The income that he received from this extra job was ridiculous because teachers were still extremely badly paid. In addition, he had practically no spare time, not even at weekends. Nonetheless, he considered the sacrifice worthwhile because for the first time in his life he discovered the happiness that work can provide.

Januário feels very comfortable teaching Portuguese, even if only to the most backward classes. Not just because of his natural inclination to teach but also because of his passion for reading. In fact, he devours everything he can lay his hands on – magazines, scientific books, fiction. Everything temporarily satisfies his insatiable thirst for reading. A voracious need that barely permits him to separate the wheat from the chaff, but which helps him a great deal as a teacher. His enthusiasm cannot but be transferred to his students. These, in the majority, are men and women, tired after a whole day at work, still hungry after the unvaried daily meal of *ushua* and cabbage, depressed by the prospect of having to walk back to their homes outside town, where nothing awaits them besides the following day's worries. Despite this, Januário manages to astonish them with the hidden logic of grammar, the rhythm of a verse or the beauty of a sentence, awakening in them a desire to master a language that they did not drink in with their mother's milk.

These small successes awoke in Januário a creative initiative that had lain dormant from years of routine work. It allowed him to develop truly original teaching methods in a school where the majority of the night-school teachers approached their activity as another painful task to add to their daily stress and frustrations. So it had been his idea to organise a literary contest for the night students, with appealing prizes – domestic utensils, clothing and food – everything arranged at great cost. The jury was made up of four teachers of Portuguese and a journalist who had aspirations to being a literary critic, especially invited because of his reputation. Januário, as organiser of the contest, was also part of the jury. This meant that for two whole months he had been obliged to wake up at dawn to read the work of the contestants.

When the members of the jury finally gathered to decide how to award the prizes, the journalist wanted, from the outset, to impose his will over the timid night-school teachers. Januário tried to confront him but received no support from his colleagues who seemed won over by the journalist's authoritative soliloquies. And so, under the influence of the journalist, the prizes were awarded to writers of short stories and poems without substance, whose originality consisted only in the fact of being written in a language so refined and hermetic as to be unintelligible. Januário, who frequently challenged the journalist's opinion, openly declared that he could not understand what the authors chosen by that scribe wanted to say in their obscure rhetoric. The other man, with a saccharine smile, would simply excuse himself from repeating his 'infallible' arguments, which perhaps Januário, he would say with a hint of contempt, had not understood. The other teachers, scared perhaps of being branded by the same contempt, would hasten to agree with him.

'That journalist ruined everything. And my colleagues . . . I almost feel ashamed for them,' Januário tells Leia. 'And the worst of it is that there were some really good works entered, which deserved a prize. I don't know what the students will think.'

'Forget it. Next time don't invite any literary critical journalists,' says Leia, trying to console him.

'I am so fed up that, for me, there will be no next time. I don't think it is possible to do anything in this country, not even the simplest things, because of the arrogance of all the one-eyed kings. They're useless but they think they're great.'

'I'm sorry. The idea of the contest was such a lovely one!' laments Leia, nestling deeper into her husband's arms, while he caresses her face distractedly, aware that the midnight news has begun. The voice of the newsreader reports more massacres, more appeals to the international community to support those affected and displaced by the natural and man-made disasters that ravage the country.

'One of these days I'm going to give up listening to the radio. It's all so sad . . .' says Leia.

Januário doesn't respond. The newsreader, indifferent and calm, reports on the huge success in Europe of the Mozambican National Singing and Dancing Company.

'You see, not everything is so sad. Look at the success of the National Company overseas. Indeed, I think the only richness this country now has lies in its culture, its art. The Mozambican is a born artist!' comments Januário with a touch of pride in his voice. 'It's just that unfortunately the artist is not recognised as he deserves to be.'

Suddenly, the memory of something he witnessed recently at the airport comes into his mind. Out of curiosity, he had peeped into the VIP lounge where he had recognised two government ministers. They were reclining without a care in the world on comfortable sofas, surrounded by assistants with whom they were chatting and laughing, while the protocol officials were silently taking care of their luggage. At the same time, the artist Malangatana was patiently waiting for his turn in the check-in queue, before carrying his luggage to the common departure area with difficulty.

The scene had stuck in his mind because, he thought, in years to come almost nobody will remember the unconcerned ministers whom he saw gossiping in the VIP lounge. On the other hand, the name and the works of Malangatana will possibly endure forever.

'It's bullshit – artists in this country are not recognised at all. Maybe even those fine dancers at the national dance company are almost starving, maybe they don't even earn enough money to buy mackerel,' concludes Januário sadly when he has finished telling Leia about this episode. Leia, already half asleep, hardly listens to him. She is roused, though, alarmed, by the whimpers of little Iris who seems about to wake up again.

'I think she's calmed down,' Leia sighs, relieved, when a little later the child stops groaning. 'It's already so late and I need to sleep well. Tomorrow I have many things to do. Did I tell you that I am going to Atalia's to use her sewing machine? Maybe I'll be able to make two small dresses for Iris who's running out of clothes. It's good, isn't it?'

Januário smiles. For him, one of Leia's greatest charms is her capacity to feel happiness about such simple things as going to sew her daughter's clothes at her friend Atalia's house.

'It's good, yes, it's very good,' he says, with tenderness, moving around in bed to find the best position in which to sleep.

Leia, beside him, has just fallen into a deep sleep.

In the home of Mena and Dupont

At last the South Africans have arrived. One of them is really a South African Boer by birth. He has the large build and rough facial features of the Boers. He looks older than forty, but is actually much younger. What makes him seem older is the volume of his flesh, at once strangely slack and compact, which appears to fill the sofa on which he is seated.

Within the military, he specialises in actions of destabilisation against Mozambique and Angola, which began immediately after they became independent. This is not the first time he has undertaken an operation inside Mozambique, which is why he faces the mission to be accomplished before dawn with the greatest serenity. He just wishes it could be over quickly because, if everything goes as planned, he will be given an extra week's holiday. And there, in his house with a swimming pool, surrounded by a garden, his chubby white wife and his chubby two-year-old son are waiting for him. He also wishes he could be rid of the three Mozambicans who, in that small room, seem to steal his air and his space. He gives thanks to his white god that he cannot understand what they are saying because this means he can isolate himself from them mentally, even if he is forced to bear their physical presence. He tries, nevertheless, not to see them, fixing his colourless eyes, sunken in fatness, on the door in front of him or on his comrade, Rui, who has come with him.

Rui is South African by acquired nationality and conviction but was born in Mozambique thirty-eight years ago. At that time his father was the head of an administrative office, in Sofala. His mother was a woman whose beauty had vanished over long years of submission to her husband and through problems with the children she bore without fail every two years. Husband and wife both belonged to families with an established tradition in Portugal, but the fortune and the assets that they were accumulating had tied them increasingly to Mozambique.

The children were raised as if they were owners of the land they were treading on. And of all of them, Rui was always the most conscious of that 'right of possession'. He was also the most handsome of her brood. 'What a beautiful young boy,' exclaimed her friends when he was still a child. 'What a handsome man,' they think today when they see him.

Rui is truly a good-looking man, even if his is a cruel beauty and he is a little blasé. His tall body still conserves the proportions and feline grace of a twenty-year-old. And his face, with features at once delicate and masculine, tanned by an intense life in the open air, is almost a miracle of proportion.

Only very discerning women do not allow themselves to be seduced, because only they perceive the deep cruelty that lies within his honey-coloured eyes and the cruel turn of his disdainful mouth. But Rui wants nothing to do with discerning women. All he wants in a woman is an attractive body and a certain refinement of manners that has nothing to do with intelligence. Above all he likes women who don't expect too much and have a sense of fair play; women who will release him from an affair without rancour or unpleasant scenes. That is why, despite his mother plaguing him about the need to start a family, he remains single, and single he wishes to stay until the end of his days. 'This bird doesn't want a cage. He has been like this since he was a kid,' his father always says, not without a hint of admiration, because he himself would have preferred not to have been snared in the web of a breeding woman.

The best moments of Rui's life from his childhood onwards were spent in complete freedom, hunting wild animals or fishing in the streams that flowed near his house. Much later, as a high school student in Lourenço Marques, he alleviated the tedium of books with memories of exciting buffalo and lion hunts, which he had undertaken with his father during the holidays.

On finishing high school, he refused to continue his studies, opposing his parents' plans for him to become a doctor or an engineer. He was never actually a bad student, but the discipline of study conflicted with his adventurous nature. So having finished high school, he was happy to begin making his dream of starting a safari business in Mozambique come true, and he did so with the support of some rich South Africans, who also loved hunting.

Rui left his company's administrative matters entirely in the hands of his trusted employees and accompanied his clients in person to the hunting reserves. His experience with wild animals over many years – he was also a very good shot – allowed him to offer them experiences beyond their dreams.

His fame as an eminent hunter and for the efficiency of his enterprise spread rapidly through the hunting world. So before he was thirty, Rui had already become a rich man, only concerned with greedily enjoying the good things of life.

The independence of Mozambique took him by surprise because, though he knew that *terrs* existed in the north of the colony, he had not realised how determined they were. Moreover, by using bribes, he had been able to escape military service, despite his athletic build and perfect health. And because Frelimo targeted the army and other direct agents of colonial power, he had never had to come face to face with people who were often described as a bunch of tattered ruffians.

Indeed, Rui hardly gave credence to the *terrs*, not only because they moved in another world, but because he had confidence in Kaúlza de Arriaga's 'Gordian Knot',[1], a military campaign of ruthless violence, which was said to exterminate the *terrs* quickly, like so much vermin. Not even when his friends, after a few whiskies, told him in fearful tones about coffins being shipped to Portugal did he take Frelimo seriously. He never gave a second thought to such whispered rumours; after all the coffins contained the corpses of lowly Portuguese soldiers, forced to enlist and fight in the bush.

So, immediately after the coup d'état of 25 April in Portugal, when Frelimo claimed Mozambican independence, Rui did not take this action seriously. He only began to realise that such talk was not frivolous when the Portuguese government, after various prolonged manoeuvres, agreed to enter into discussions on the subject. Then, for a while, Rui fell into a sort of daze, aware only of a permanent sensation of helplessness and unreality.

Nevertheless, it was not in his nature to give up easily. So he quickly joined the under-cover movements which were fighting to preserve settler rule. And so it was that on 7 September[2] Rui was among the mob that stormed the Radio Club, took it over and undertook a real hunt for black people. He alone killed

[1] Gordian Knot – a military campaign by the head of military operations in Mozambique from 1969, Kaúlza de Arriaga, to isolate Frelimo by creating protected villages. His means were ruthless and exceedingly violent.
[2] 7 September – date in 1974 when reactionary Portuguese settlers attempted a coup d'état in Lourenço Marques.

eighty-two blacks, whom he counted coldly, one by one as he picked them off. On that day he neither ate nor drank, sustained by his hatred and the intense pleasure that the hunt inspired in him. So it was with a sensation of triumph that he managed to get away like a cat from the multitude of angry blacks who were avenging their dead, and killing with knives and stones any white person they encountered.

Despite the trail of blood that 7 September left in its wake, it was simply a desperate attempt to stop the course of history and, contrary to what its architects had planned, it failed. Rui, like so many other Portuguese, abandoned Mozambique immediately after the conspiracy.

He fled to South Africa, where he could count on friends to help him divert his assets, and wasted no time in becoming involved in South Africa's destabilisation plans against Mozambique. In the beginning there was support for armed groups specialising in the massacre of defenceless civilians and in the unbridled destruction of the social and economic infrastructure. And more recently he has himself joined the South African commandos who, periodically, undertake murderous raids in Maputo and Matola.

The raid in which Rui is about to participate is, compared with previous ones, of minor importance. It entails murdering a married couple who are living in a flat next to one occupied by members of the African National Congress. It has to appear as if the attackers have mistaken the target of their action, because the objective of their mission is to provoke insecurity and panic among the population and anger against the Mozambican government for supporting the ANC.

The job would hold almost no interest for Rui were it not for the risk of undertaking an exploit in the heart of the city. The last one he participated in sent eight people to the other world and he enjoyed himself very much – painting himself black and wearing a uniform identical to that of the Mozambican army.

'What about a whisky, mister?' Dupont asked him suddenly.

Rui mechanically took the proffered glass from the owner of the house.

'Ice, mister?'

'One block.'

'Soda?'

'Just ice.'

Despite being nervous and upset by the late arrival and crude manners of the South Africans, Dupont still forces a smile and offers a whisky to the fat South African. His refusal is so categorical that Dupont almost drops the glass.

'This shit is really crapping himself because of the South Africans,' Romu thinks to himself, observing the scene in an amused way. But even he does not feel completely at ease in the presence of the two South Africans, who are either silent or exchange rough words in Afrikaans. Zalíua continues to chain-smoke, filling the ashtrays to overflowing with butts and the room with stale smoke. He, too, does not feel completely at ease.

Meanwhile, in the kitchen, Mena awaits her husband's order to serve dinner. Everything has been standing for so long that she is no longer hungry. All she wants to do is lie down on her bed and sleep a deep sleep disconnecting her from a reality so laden with foreboding.

'Go on, you can serve dinner now. Is everything ready?' asks Dupont, suddenly bursting into the kitchen and nervously examining the contents of the pots.

'No curry and *matapa*. Only meat, potato and salad,' he ordered her that morning. And Mena cooked only meat, lots of meat, bought at Interfranca with the mysterious foreign currency that her husband now flaunts.

'You can bring the salad now. Then fetch the rest later,' says Dupont, hurrying his wife out of the kitchen.

'What a handsome man,' she thinks on seeing Rui when she enters the room. 'What a piece of mulatto,' thinks Rui to himself when he sees her.

For a very brief instant, their gazes meet appreciatively before Mena hurriedly puts the salad bowl on the table and leaves, murmuring a faint 'good evening'. The 'real South African' does not even bother to respond. Rui, though, answers the greeting with an unexpectedly caressing smile.

The impression Mena has made on one of the recent arrivals does not pass Dupont by and he is perplexed to realise that the jealousy he feels contains an element of self-satisfaction. Satisfaction because a white South African admires his woman.

Romu also notices Rui's appreciative gaze and almost suffocates with resentment and indignation.

'That Boer son-of-a-bitch digs the chick. There's no apartheid when it suits them. And the chick is also all . . . bitch.'

When, a little later, Mena comes in again with serving dishes piled up with meat and potatoes, the silence that hangs in the room is almost palpable. Still, perturbed by Rui's gaze, after placing everything on the sideboard, she stands and waits for her husband to invite his guests to eat.

'Misters, please, dinner is served,' Dupont announces, all smiles. It still does not enter his head to introduce his wife to the newcomers.

The 'real South African' carries on staring at the door in front of him. Rui speaks for the two of them: 'We've already eaten,' he says.

'What . . . already eaten?' responds the owner of the house, surprised.

'We ate before coming,' repeats the other laconically.

'It can't be. It was arranged that you would eat here. We

107

waited for the misters until this hour. It's already past eleven o'clock and the misters don't eat. The food is good. Good meat of Interfranca, misters. You can't do this . . . no.'

Rui abstains from further explanation and instead fixes his eyes on Mena who witnesses the whole scene with a mixture of shame and irony.

'Well, we'll eat our supper then,' says Romu, the first to overcome the embarrassing situation.

Zalíua finishes smoking the cigarette he has in his mouth and then sits down at the table, followed by Mena. Dupont is the last one to take a seat, waiting in case the South Africans change their minds. They, however, continue to lounge on the sofas, the 'real South African' with an absent air, and Rui watching the lady of the house as if no one else was in the room. At table, Mena barely touches her food and Dupont has also lost his appetite. He is only sorry he has wasted money on a sumptuous banquet that the South Africans, having arrived two hours late, refuse to eat. Only Romu and Zalíua eat the food with any pleasure.

'Mister, what about another whisky?' Dupont asks suddenly, noticing Rui's empty glass.

'This guy really is a shit,' thinks Romu, 'the only thing the Boers haven't done is spit in his face. They don't even want his food and the guy is full of politeness: mister do you want whisky, mister do you want ice . . . it makes me sick.'

Mister does not accept another whisky. He is anxious for the meal to end quickly so they can finalise the last details of the raid. As if reading his thoughts, the 'real South African' asks in Afrikaans:

'When are they going to finish eating? There's not much time.'

'I think they are finishing.'

'Let's see! When the kaffirs start eating they never finish,' comments the other.

'It's true . . . But the girl is quite beautiful,' says Rui, almost without wanting to.

The other cannot believe his ears and responds with indignant surprise.

'Beautiful?'

He stares again at the door in front of him, ruminating on his comrade's comment. For him Mena is nothing but a shadow, someone who, according to the divine laws of his god, only exists to serve the white man. This is what he has been taught from childhood and this is the way he wants it to stay. To appreciate a coloured! It is quite obvious to him that the perverted blood of the Portuguese runs in Rui's veins.

What the 'real South African' does not know is that Rui is surprised at himself. The type of woman to whom he is normally attracted has to be white, and preferably, blonde. This mulatto though, undoubtedly attracts him, even if against his will.

'Clear the table quickly,' orders Dupont, a little later, as soon as the silent meal has ended.

Mena notices that her husband's hands are shaking and hears, in his voice, a touch of fear. Anxious, she rushes to clear the table, feeling Rui's gaze upon her. When she finally leaves with a brief 'Good evening,' she dares to look straight at him. And it is then that she catches, in the perfect face, his latent cruelty.

'Go and rest, go,' Dupont says to her, pushing her nervously out of the room and then inviting the South Africans to sit at the table, which has been cleared of plates and cutlery.

The five men, bent over maps and papers, now take care of the final details of the raid for that morning, with Rui acting as interpreter, as he is the only one who speaks Portuguese, English and a little Afrikaans. They are so absorbed that none of them notices the quiet creak as Mena pushes the door very slightly ajar. Through the imperceptible gap, she manages to understand that the five men in her living room are preparing to commit murder. She also manages to understand that the victims live somewhere in Emília Daússe Avenue and that they are to be eliminated at about one o'clock in the morning.

Mena does not know the details of the plan but what she has been able to gather through the gap in the door leaves her in such extreme anguish that she stumbles to her room where she lies down without getting undressed. Only then does she realise that she forgot to close the living room door. But she does not move because she is no longer afraid of anything, and nothing matters any more.

When Dupont, some time later, bursts into the room, out of breath, Mena lies waiting for him to interrogate her over the door. He, however, seems to have noticed nothing. Thinking at first that she is asleep, he fails to repress a gesture of scared surprise when he sees her wide-open eyes fixed upon him.

'Are you still awake?' he asks, mechanically, as he finishes putting on the anorak he has taken out of the wardrobe.

Mena again notices his hand shaking and the touch of fear in his voice and doesn't answer.

'I'm going out, but I'll be back soon,' he says hurriedly.

'Don't go. Please don't go,' Mena says, making a great effort to articulate the words.

'Why? We're just going for a walk!' lies Dupont, half-puzzled.

'Don't go,' she repeats.

Mena wants to tell him that she knows what is going to happen in some house in Emília Daússe Avenue. But she lacks the energy either to say anything or to listen to justifications, as her words have stopped forming a connecting bridge between herself and the man who is observing her so suspiciously. Even so, expecting some miracle perhaps, she begs him one last time:

'Don't go. Please don't go.'

Irritated, Dupont turns his back and rushes out of the room, forgetting to switch off the light. Mena follows him with her eyes.

Moments later, a sudden silence tells her she is alone in the house. Dupont and the others have left and are on their way to find their victims.

01.00 HOURS

In the home of Narguiss

What kind of force is it that prevents her from getting up and running to her Abdul who, already impatient, is kicking the door almost off its hinges. 'No shout . . . wait only little,' she begs, shaking out of fear that he will leave her again. But Abdul doesn't leave, he continues kicking the door and screaming as if someone outside was harming him. And she is not able to open the door. It's so close, only a few steps away, a few, so few that when she finds she cannot stand up she decides to crawl. Fighting against the force that is almost paralysing her, she progresses with a slowness that makes Abdul's screams unbearable. Almost there . . . a little more . . . now just to raise her arm, reach the lock and turn the key . . . once, twice. But her arm is too heavy . . . so heavy . . . she can't . . . no . . .

Narguiss wakes up sweating, despite the May mists that are filtering in through the screen door that opens from the kitchen onto the balcony. 'Final everything to be a dream . . . Abdul not come,' she laments, looking disappointedly around her. It was a terrible dream, but Abdul was in it. It was better than being alone like that, without husband, on day of Eid.

She does not remember having fallen asleep, seated with her arms on the kitchen table. She remembers, though, the nightmare from which she has just emerged and the strange sensation of having seen Abdul through the door, which he was kicking because his hands were full of parcels.

'But he all a dream, really. Abdul not here,' she groans softly. She tries to move her legs and arms and realises, relieved, that they obey her perfectly. Everything was really just a dream.

Abdul has not come and nothing restricts her movements. But
... the screams and the strange noise that come from the road
are not a dream. They are real, and cut the silence of the
morning in a frightening way.

Curious, Narguiss rolls her immense body to the screen door
and goes onto the balcony. At first she doesn't want to believe
what she sees. She even believes she has fallen into another
nightmare, so strange does everything seem to her.

On the balcony of the first floor, just in front of her, the
couple who live there and who she just knows by sight, sway
together, screaming. She screams for help and he, wrapped in
what seems to be a sheet, repeats something that Narguiss
cannot understand. Now and again he also screams for help.

Despite the darkness of the moonless night, Narguiss can see
them perfectly, illuminated by spotlights controlled from the
road. Suddenly they begin running from one side to the other of
the tiny balcony in a macabre dance.

Narguiss does not know if the bullets that hit them come
from inside their house or from the men with the spotlight who
are also firing continuously. But when she sees them falling, she
begins to scream.

'They kills people ... *muanene inluco* ... they kills people
... there ... *muanene inluco* ...'

She does not see the man who, from the street, points his gun
at her because her entire attention is centred on the balcony of
the flat in front of her. The carefully placed bullets hit her in her
neck and in her chest and she is amazed by the sensation of
infinite peace that accompanies her when she falls. Nothing can
make her suffer any more, neither Eid without the moon, nor
her unmarried daughters, nor even Abdul.

As if her immense body refuses to give up, she turns around
and, sliding down slowly, Narguiss falls at last into a sitting
position with her back leaning against the bars of the balcony

railing. And that is how, a little later, her daughters, alerted by the screams and by the shots, find her.

In the home of Leia and Januário

At first it seemed like only a slight scratching but slowly it has become a syncopated noise, which Leia tries, in vain, to identify. In her little bed beside them, her daughter is still in an agitated sleep, whimpering, and now and again tossing and turning. Januário, meanwhile, rests peacefully, lying on his stomach and holding his pillow with both hands, as is his habit. Leia hesitates to wake him, the more so when it seems as if the noise has stopped. She tries to find sleep again, blaming everything on her taut nerves. The noise, though, returns and this time it is clearer and more insistent.

'Januário, can you hear?' she whispers to her husband who doesn't wake up.

She repeats the question a few times, a little more loudly each time, and ends up by shaking him violently. Januário wakes up bewildered and begs her to let him sleep.

'Someone is messing around with our front door,' insists Leia, with nervous impatience.

He tries to calm her down, reminding her, half ironically, that only very professional burglars would be able to break the very secure bars left, fortuitously, by the friends who had rented them the flat. Besides that, they own nothing that could tempt burglars. But, as soon as he has spoken, he sits up in bed, alert and tense.

'You're right,' he agrees. 'Someone is trying to get in.'

117

Leia moves to switch on the bedside light but Januário, his eyes already used to the darkness, stops her with a gesture.

'I'll go and see what it is,' he says in a whisper, leaving the room on tip-toe.

Leia warns him to be careful and remains in bed, watching her daughter sleep. She feels a biting chill down her spine, a sign of fear from when she was a child. Her husband's absence feels like an eternity and when he finally returns she, who knows him so well, can see that he is very perturbed.

To his wife's anxious questions, Januário replies that no, they do not seem to be burglars. Hidden in a corner of the hall that opens from the front door, he is able to distinguish two men. They have already broken open the wooden door and are now trying to tear out the bars. One of them has a gun in his right hand and in the other holds a torch, in the light of which the second man works on the bars. The most frightening thing is that this one is a white man.

Leia understands the implications of her husband's words because attacks on ANC refugees are common. Just recently, eight such people were killed in Matola. The South African commando unit came, killed, and left with impunity. Nothing happened to them. And now . . .

'It must be the people next door that they're after,' murmurs Leia, referring to the ANC refugees who are their neighbours.

'What do you want me to do? Go and tell them that actually it's not us they're supposed to kill?'

'I don't know . . . I . . . I just know that I don't want to die because of those ANC cadres.'

The chill down her spine is like ice. It felt like this during her final school exams and again when she gave birth. And now it is almost unbearable.

'I'm scared, Januário. I'm so scared,' she moans, clinging to her husband.

Januário feels her shivering in his arms and hates himself for not being able to decide what to do because, in his disorientation, he cannot think straight.

'And our daughter? And our daughter? They think that we are ANC and will kill the child too,' sobs Leia.

Slowly, very slowly, Januário releases himself from her and leaves the room. At the same time he feels an overwhelming desire to vomit:

'ANC other flat. We Mozambicans. We Mozambicans,' he shouts, cursing his poor English.

He feels a complete bastard but continues shouting at the two men who, taken by surprise, stop for a moment from their work on the very secure bars. Januário, confident about having enlightened them about what he supposes is a mistake, approaches the door. It is then that the first man shines the torch on him with one hand and tries to shoot him with the other: quiet, dull shots, like corks popping out of champagne bottles.

'They have silencers on their guns,' Januário realises, shaking.

He returns to the bedroom and, without a word, picks up his daughter who is now sleeping peacefully and hides her under the bed. He then runs to the small balcony off the living room, dragging Leia by the hand. It is his intention to alert the neighbours before the South Africans (because he is certain they are South Africans) are able to break into their apartment.

Barefoot, Leia in her nightie and he wrapped in a sheet thrown hurriedly over his underpants, scream in desperation, in the cold morning. They only become aware of the spotlights and that they are being shot at from the street at the same moment as the two men, who have just broken down the bars on the front door, burst into the room. Caught between gunshot from two sides, there is nowhere to run.

Falling, Leia only thinks that tomorrow she will no longer go and sew at her friend Atalia's, and Januário is surprised to find that he no longer feels fear, but only great anger at being so young, yet about to die.

In the home of Mena and Dupont

'Please, that's what I said, it's not a mistake. They're going to kill someone in Emília Daússe Avenue. The murderers left from here, from my house. Listen . . . hello . . . hello . . .' insists Mena, in despair.

She has a clear sensation that at the other end of the line the man, who says he is the officer-in-charge of the police station, isn't taking her seriously. Besides, she herself is aware how unreal her words sound. But she doesn't give up trying to convince the man listening to her, who limits himself to repeating 'correct . . . going to kill . . . correct . . .' in a slow, slurred voice that upsets her.

Immediately after Dupont and the others had left, Mena ran to the phone and looked for the number of a police station in the telephone directory. It was then that she discovered how difficult it is to get through to a police station either because the line is engaged or because no one answers or simply because the line is dead. And now that finally she has someone on the line she feels that that her desperate persistence has been in vain.

'Listen sir . . . you must send someone immediately. The murderers are already there . . . are you listening? . . . Hello . . .'

'Correct . . . they're going to kill . . . correct . . .' the slow, slurred voice answers her.

Mena is now sure that the man not only doubts what she is

120

saying, but is also drunk. The temptation to hang up the phone is enormous. Instead, she repeats very carefully, and as if speaking to a child, everything she has been saying for the past five minutes. Suddenly, she feels as if no one is listening at the other end of the line.

This is, in fact, the case. The officer-in-charge did not respond to Mena's urgent tone, which sounded to him like a mosquito buzzing, and fell asleep over the desk, letting the phone fall from his hand. He is now sleeping off the drunkenness caused by several glasses of *tontonto*, swallowed in a rush before going to work. The only sustenance he has had today is the daily diet of *ushua* and cabbage, and the alcohol has now rendered him quite incapable of answering the telephone again.

Luckily, Mena cannot see him straddled on a precarious chair that looks as if it could collapse at any moment under his weight, his face smothered in the dust on the desk, and the telephone, hanging on its cord, swinging at his side. Nevertheless, he is not out of place with all that surrounds him, poorly lit by the only bulb on the ceiling, misted by dust and fly excrement. The walls, once painted white, are now of an indefinite colour somewhere between grey and an oily brown. On a bare floor that is full of holes, cockroaches take their nocturnal walks. They emerge from two cupboards with broken glass doors onto the very desk of the officer-in-charge.

Mena sees nothing of this but knows that she can expect no help from the drunken man on whom she has lost precious time. Seated on the floor, next to the telephone table, she is close to giving up – after all she does not even know the unfortunate ones who are going to die, nor why they are going to die, far away on Emília Daússe Avenue. A sensation of such impotence invades her that she puts the telephone directory away – then immediately pulls it out again and begins to page through it, feverishly looking for the number of another police station. She can hardly believe it when finally, someone at the other end of the line answers her calmly, almost politely. Someone who, despite her refusing to identify herself, seems to take her report seriously, asks pertinent and interested questions and who, at last, leaves her almost convinced that everything will be done to prevent the crime. Only then does Mena relax. At the same time she becomes aware of a great lassitude. Despite this, she does not go to bed. She drags herself onto one of the sofas in the living room and lies there waiting . . . waiting . . .

08.00 HOURS

The Dead and the Living

The home of Narguiss is no longer the home of Narguiss. Narguiss is dead. Her immense body now rests in the morgue where the police took it and where an autopsy will be done. It was removed from her house about half an hour ago amid the loud screaming and wailing of her eldest daughters, Fauzia and some of the neighbours.

Only Muntaz understood the necessity of an autopsy, since her mother's death had been a crime. And it was Muntaz who, as a medical student, asked that the autopsy be done urgently so that the body could be returned home that morning, because it is only there that it can be prepared in accordance with the Muslim rituals of the dead. Then the experienced women will come, who will bathe the body of Narguiss, press down on her internal organs until the cleaning water comes out clean, free of any impurities, and, finally, wrap her in an immaculate white cloth which serves as the shroud. All this will be done by the experienced women, but meanwhile the body still rests in the morgue.

Here, at home, lying on Narguiss' big bed are her three daughters, completely covered by *capulanas*, swaying under the influence of sedatives, between sleepiness and pain. Seated on the grass mats that are spread out on the floor for the mourners are the women who have begun to arrive, mostly neighbours from the same building who appear hastily, awakened in the early morning by the shooting in the street. They come partly out of compassion and partly out of curiosity, eager to know the details of this strange crime. All of them leave their shoes at

125

the entrance of the room and burst in, crying, going to the bed where the three girls are resting, kissing them and hugging them, with great lamentations. Then without another tear, they settle on the grass mats, sitting in mournful silence or exchanging comments in low, sorrowful voices.

The men are in the living room and, as the *moulana* has still not arrived to say the prayers, they discuss the crime. They consider it intriguing that the murderers came with spotlights, showing obvious contempt for the country's security forces. The fast reaction of the police also seems curious: even if it did not prevent the victims being killed, their arrival at least stopped the assailants from getting away. Beyond this each of them expresses puzzled, contradictory opinions. They are, though, all in agreement on one point: 'The government must send away the ANC cadres. Otherwise they must find them an isolated place to stay, because it is very dangerous to live near them.'

In the bedroom the women share this view while lamenting that Narguiss, a woman who never wanted anything to do with politics, had to die. And Fauzia cannot refrain from saying: 'I told them to go to Portugal. I really warned them . . .'

◆

The home of Leia and Janúario is no longer the home of Leia and Janúario. Leia is dead. Janúario is dead.

The police found their bodies riddled with bullets, slumped on the balcony. Lying down on top of them, covered in blood, was little Iris. She could neither speak nor cry, and her eyes, which were wide open, seem fixed on a point beyond human reach.

Luckily for the police, the neighbour, a clear-headed and helpful woman from the second floor, arrived and lifted the child off her parents. She took her to the bathroom where she washed and dressed her without the child showing the slightest reaction. When, finally, she brought her down to the living room, the police were already preparing to leave, disappointed at having no one from the family to interrogate other than a silent child with a lost, blank gaze.

The neighbour from the second floor simply took the little girl back to her flat until the arrival of Leia's family who had already been informed of the crime. Now there is no one in Leia and Janúario's home, not even the bodies, which have already been taken to the morgue. All that remains is the modest furniture made of formica and cheap wood, bought second-hand, and, in one corner, the many little pots of African violets and the beautiful Mecufi mat which, indifferent to the tragedy that has befallen the home, continue to give a touch of refinement and freshness to the still room.

◆

The home of Mena and Dupont is no longer the home of Mena and Dupont. Dupont is dead.

Mena is curled up on one of the artificial leather sofas that clutter the room. She concentrates all her attention on the Xirico radio that she holds in both hands. The news, though, proceeds without a single word about any crime in Emília Daússe Avenue. Disappointed, she puts the radio on the floor and pulls the blanket up a little higher. She is cold, a cold that has intensified during her interminable vigil, waiting for she knows not what.

Since hanging up the telephone after her last contact with the police, she has been curled up on the artificial leather sofa, covered with a velvety blanket, one side a red and purple design, the other an imitation leopard skin. It is an old blanket, a wedding present from a group of friends from Angoche which, because it was so precious, has never been used. Having been for so long locked in a damp cupboard, it emits an unpleasant smell of mildew. But Mena prefers the smell to covering herself with a blanket from her bed, impregnated with the smell of Dupont.

Now that she is aware of the depths of ignominy to which her husband can sink, she is surprised at herself for having coped for so long with his smell, his tiring displays of jealousy, his beatings, his prickliness over money, his rushed, greedy way of making love. She asks herself where he can be now, why he has not yet returned home, and if the victims have managed to escape . . . That is the reason for her anguish, the pain of not knowing, and of not being able to ask anything. Sometimes a desire to call the last police station she contacted floods over her, but an inexplicable fear prevents her from doing so. Fear, perhaps, of being told the truth by a voice without a face, which would make it all the more frightening.

And that is why she still does not know that the last officer she spoke to, the one with the polite calm voice, believed her report and immediately sent a patrol to Emília Daússe Avenue. It was not difficult to find the scene of the crime and, while the patrol had not arrived in time to prevent it, they managed to intercept the killers who were just about to run away. Then, in the midst of the ensuing gunfight, Dupont was fatally wounded.

Mena only now realises that the room is filled with light. Besides feeling cold, she feels a strange lethargy, which only affects her body because her mind is more awake and alert than ever. She is surprised not to feel hungry despite the long hours of vigil and although she ate hardly any dinner. On the contrary a sensation of bloatedness almost prevents her from breathing. Yet she longs for her morning cup of coffee.

She gets up and goes to the kitchen to make it, then she drinks the beverage as she has done every morning, steaming hot and without sugar. This is a habit she acquired when she was single, and one that Dupont never understood. 'What an obsession – drinking coffee, first thing in the morning,' he would taunt.

Mena sips the hot, bitter drink with the same pleasure as always, only now she can enjoy it freely. Dupont is not there to mock her, nobody is in the empty house. Her companion is the sense of interminable waiting, so tangible it almost hangs in the air.

She almost drops the coffee cup when she notices that it is only a few seconds before the nine o'clock news. She picks up the Xirico radio from the floor and listens to it in feverish anxiety . . . This time the radio reports: 'At about one o'clock this morning a commando unit made up of South Africans and Mozambicans murdered three citizens at Emília Daússe Avenue. The names of the victims are Janúario Mario Moveia and his wife Leia Percina Moveia, and Narguiss Selemane. The couple leaves a daughter of two years old and Mrs Selemane leaves a husband and three daughters. Apparently the target of the attackers were ANC members who live in a flat next door to the unfortunate couple. Thanks to the prompt intervention of our security forces, three of the attackers were captured and two were shot dead when they tried to resist arrest. Meanwhile investigations continue to find out the circumstances surrounding the crime.'

The official reading of the report comes to an end. Mena switches off the radio and rises from the sofa, unable to bear the tension weighing down on her. So the police did not arrive in time to prevent a crime . . . but at least they arrested the killers . . . two are dead, might Dupont be one of them? she asks herself while pacing back and forth.

Mena surprises herself because – having lived for so many years with this man, having slept with him, and having suffered with him and from him – in a moment like this her heart is empty of any feeling, even hatred. She does not even feel remorse at having denounced him. She just feels, for the first time, that she holds her life in her hands, a life that belongs completely to her because, even if Dupont is still alive, it will no longer be possible for her to live with him.

She fetches more coffee and warms her frozen hands on the cup while sipping it slowly. She already feels slightly nauseous as the bitter fluid reaches her empty stomach. Still with the cup in her hand, she goes into her bedroom and, looking into the mirror, her eyes painful and dry from insomnia, she realises that she has aged several years overnight. But she no longer feels cold and her earlier lethargy has given way to an anxious wish to move about, to do something, something that will delay the moment of thinking about what is to become of her life – before her lies the unknown, which is at once attractive and frightening.

A prolonged warm shower refreshes her and for a brief moment gives her the calmness necessary to proceed with the ritual of dressing and of putting on make-up, which she does with painstaking care. Despite not being hungry she forces herself to swallow a glass of milk and tries to eat a slice of bread, which she cannot finish. Leaving the table, she feels compelled to pace back and forth, back and forth again and again. She only stops when the doorbell rings. She is not surprised when, on opening the door, she is faced by two unknown men, and one of them says to her:

'We are from the police. Is this the house of Virgilio Dupont?'

'Yes it is,' answers Mena, suddenly feeling very calm.

'Ma'am, are you his wife?' asks the same man, who has the strange sensation that the woman who has answered the door has been waiting for him for a long time.

'Yes I am,' she confirms.

'We would like you to accompany us. It seems your husband has a problem. Your presence is required, ma'am, we need you just to make a statement,' says the man with professional subtlety.

'I know. My husband is implicated in the crime of Emília Daússe Avenue.'

'You . . . you know, ma'am?' asks the policeman, taken aback by this beautiful woman who tells him, spontaneously, that her husband is involved in a crime.

'It was I who warned the police. So, shall we go? I'm just going to fetch my purse,' says Mena, returning immediately.

◆

On closing the door of her home, she knows that she is also closing the door on her past and taking the first steps towards a new and unpredictable destiny.

Glossary

ANC   African National Congress

assimilado   a non-white person who has been accepted into white Portuguese society in Portuguese East Africa (Mozambique)

bagia   delicacy made of bean flour, onion, red chilli peppers and spices

cafusa   a person who has one black parent and one mulatto or Indian parent

candonga   local word for the black market or informal market

capulanas   versatile, wrap-around cloths worn by women

caracata chima   cassava meal cooked with water and salt

'chapa cem' taxis   taxis that carry many people and stop at will

chibalo   forced labour

co-operantes   international expatriates who came to Mozambique to help build the new independent, socialist country

curandeiro   healer, medicine man

Frelimo   Front for the Liberation of Mozambique – movement against Portuguese colonialism and the ruling party after independence

gilebe   cake made of risen flour fried in sugar

IARNE   Institute for Assistance of Returnees from the Ex-colonies

jambire   a precious wood, almost black in colour

Jone   contraction of Johannesburg, the South African city renowned for its rich gold mines

machamba   plot of land used to grow food crops

machimbombo   local bus

mahaza   cream of rice flour, coconut milk, sugar and spices

mapira mucate cakes   cakes made from very small beans, crushed and cooked with coconut milk and spices

marusse   virgin

matapa   cassava leaves cooked with coconut milk and ground peanuts

mestiço   a person of mixed race

metical   unit of Mozambican currency

moulana   Muslim priest

muanene inluco   Oh, my god, my god!

nimino fish stew   dish made of cassava or sweet potato, coconut milk and red chilli peppers

quirre of fried vermicelli   a dessert made with milk, sugar and spices

Renamo   Resistencia Nacional Mozambicana

roti   unleavened bread often given a spicy filling

sanana cakes   flat cakes made of rice flour, coconut milk and sugar

sepoys   black colonial policemen

sirisiri matapa   green leaves cooked with coconut milk and peanut butter

suruma   cannabis

terrs   contraction of 'terrorists'; word used by settler regimes for the guerrillas fighting against them

tocassado   a light curry made with water, tomato, onion and dried mango

tontonto   person who has a grandparent of a different race; traditional alcoholic drink

torritorri sweets   sweets made with crushed peanuts and cooked in caramel

ushua   maize flour cooked with water, salt and coconut milk